Gun Facts and Myths

A Second Amendment Foundation Debate Book

Gun Facts and Myths:
A Second Amendment Foundation Debate Book
is published by
Merril Press, P.O. Box 1682, Bellevue, WA 98009
www.merrilpress.com
Phone: 425-454-7009
Distributed to the book trade by
Independent Publishers Group (IPG)
814 N. Franklin Street, Chicago, IL 60610
www.ipg.com
Trade Order Placement: 1-800-888-4741

FIRST EDITION

Library of Congress Cataloging-in-Publication Data

ISBN 978-0-936783-70-0

Printed in the United States of America

Introduction

Acknowledgements

Acknowledgements

This book would not have been possible if it had not been for the effort and dedication of the staff at GunFacts.info. The Second Amendment Foundation thanks you for compiling such a valuable resource and sharing your knowledge with the community.

Introduction

The debate about gun control is riddled with statistics that are constantly used to push an anti-civil rights agenda. The problem is most of them are just not true.

This book is a guide to help find you the truth about statistics and spread awareness to promote the expansion of gun rights and the culture of firearms ownership.

Concealed Carry

Estimated 16.3 Million Active Concealed Carry Permits

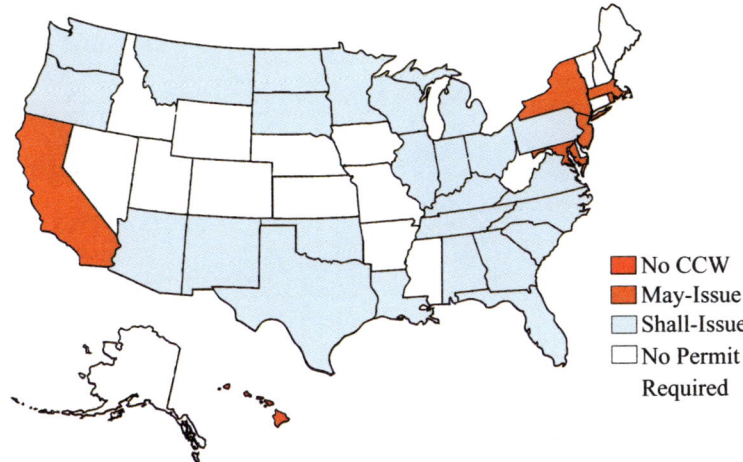

- No CCW
- May-Issue
- Shall-Issue
- No Permit Required

Myth: Concealed carry doesn't prevent crimes

Fact: News reports tell many stories of armed civilians preventing mass murder in public. A few selected at random include:

- A citizen with a gun stopped a knife-wielding man as he began stabbing people in a Salt Lake City store.
- Two men retrieved firearms from their cars and stopped a mass murder at the Appalachian School of Law.
- Citizen takes out shooter while police were pinned down in Early, Texas.
- Citizen stops apartment shoot-up in Oklahoma City.

Myth: Concealed carry laws increase crime

Concealed Carry and Violent Crime

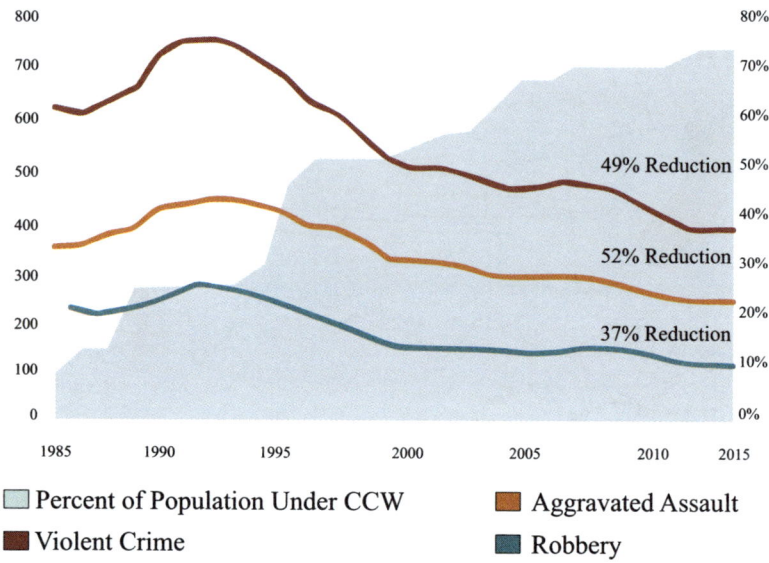

- ☐ Percent of Population Under CCW
- 🟫 Violent Crime
- 🟧 Aggravated Assault
- 🟦 Robbery

Fact: Crime rates involving gun owners with carry licenses have consistently been about 0.02% of all carry permit holders since Florida's right-to-carry law started in 1988.[1]

Fact: Forty-three states, comprising the majority of the American population, are "right-to-carry" states – thirty-six are "shall issue" states where anyone without a criminal record will be issued a permit, and seven states require no permit. In 1988 there were only ten "right-to-carry". Statistics show that in these states the crime rate fell (or did not rise) after the right-to-carry law became active (as of July, 2006).

Seven states are "may issue" states where it is nearly impossible to obtain a CCW (Concealed Carry Weapon) permit.

Fact: Gun homicides were 10% higher in states with restrictive CCW laws, according to a study spanning 1980-2009.[2]

Type of Cime	% Higher in Restrictive States
Robbery	105%
Murder	86%
Assault	82%
Violent Crime	81%
Auto Theft	60%
Rape	25%

Fact: After passing their concealed carry law, Florida's homicide rate fell from 36% above the national average to 4% below.[3]

Fact: In Texas, murder rates fell 50% faster than the national average in the year after their concealed carry law passed. Rape rates fell 93% faster in the first year after enactment, and 500% faster in the second.[4] Assaults fell 250% faster in the second year.[5]

Fact: States that disallow concealed carry have violent crime rates 11% higher than national averages.[6]

Fact: Deaths and injuries from mass public shootings fall dramatically after right-to-carry concealed handgun laws are enacted. Between 1977 and 1995,[7] the average death rate from mass shootings plummeted by up to 91% after such laws went into effect, and injuries dropped by over 80%.[8]

Fact: More to the point, crime is significantly higher in states without right-to-carry laws.[9]

Myth: Right-To-Carry laws increase violent crime 13-15%

Fact: This rather miserable working paper is a wellspring of bad methodology, which might explain why it was not (as of July 2017) published in a peer reviewed journal.

Myth: Concealed carry permit holders shoot police

Fact: The Violence Policy Center started listing instances of CCW holders shooting police.[10] From May 2007 through November 2009 (2.5 years) they recorded nine police deaths, three in one mass killing by a white supremacist using an AK-47 rifle. Of the nine, five had yet to be tried or convicted as of the date of their report.

Myth: People with concealed weapons licenses will commit crimes

Fact: The results for the first 30 states that passed "shall-issue" laws for concealed carry licenses are similar.

Fact: In Texas, citizens with concealed carry licenses are 14 times less likely to commit a crime. They are also five times less likely to commit a violent crime.[11]

State	Licenses Issued	Revoked Licenses	% Revoked	Violent Crime Rate Change
Florida	1,327,321	4,129	0.3%	-30.5%
Virginia	50,000	0	0.0%	-21.9%
Arizona	63,000	50	0.9%	-28.7%
North Carolina	59,597	1,274	1.2%	-26.4%
Minnesota	46,636	12	0.03%	8.0%
Michigan	155,000	2,178	0.1%	1.4%

Fact: People with concealed carry licenses are:[12]

- 5.7 times *less* likely to be arrested for violent offenses than the general public
- 13.5 times *less* likely to be arrested for non-violent offenses than the general public

Fact: Even gun control organizations agree it is a non-problem. One said about Texas, "because there haven't been Wild West shootouts in the streets".[13]

Fact: Of 14,000 CCW licensees in Oregon, only 4 (0.03%) were convicted of the criminal (not necessarily violent) use or possession of a firearm.

Fact: "I'm detecting that I'm eating a lot of crow on this issue ... I think that says something, that we've gotten to this point in the year and in the third largest city in America there has not been a single charge against anyone that had anything to do with a concealed handgun."[14]

Fact: In Florida, a state that has allowed concealed carry since late 1987, you are twice as likely to be attacked by an alligator as by a person with a concealed carry permit.[15]

Myth: 460 people have been killed by CCW permit holders

Fact: The "study" by gun control group Violence Policy Center covers a six-year span, meaning that at worst there is an average of 76 shootings of all types per year, including justifiable homicides.

Fact: As of 2017, there are over 14,500,000 CCW holders,[16] meaning the worst case kill rate (justifiable or not) is 0.003% of all CCW holders.

Myth: Concealed guns in bars will cause violence

Fact: In Virginia, in the first year where CCW holders were allowed to carry in bars, the number of major crimes involving firearms at bars and restaurants statewide declined 5.2%. The crimes that occurred during the law's first year were relatively minor.[17]

Myth: Texas CCW holders are arrested 66% more often

Fact: The Violence Policy Center "study" only includes arrests, not convictions.

Fact: Many of these arrests in this premature VPC "study" came in the early years of Texas CCWs when the law was not understood by most of the law enforcement community or prosecutors.

Fact: Most arrests cited are not any form of violent crime (includes bounced checks or tax delinquency).[18]

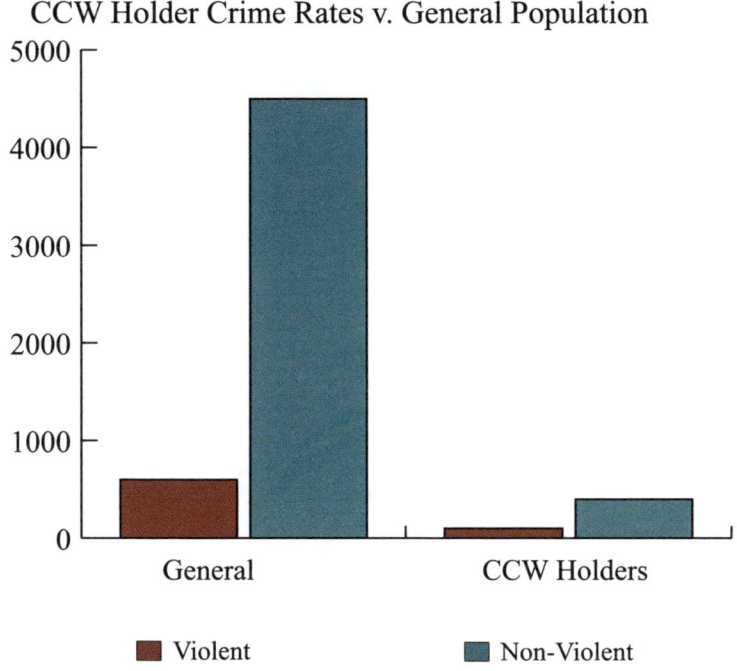

CCW Holder Crime Rates v. General Population

Fact: Compared to the entire population, Texas CCW holders are about 7.6 times less likely to be arrested for a violent crime.[19] Breakdown as follows:

- 214,000 CCW holders[20]
- 526 (0.2%) felony arrests of CCW holders that have been adjudicated
- 100 (0.05%) felony convictions

Fact: A different study concludes that the four-year violent crime arrest rate for CCW holders is 128 per 100,000. For the general population, it is 710 per 100,000. In other words, CCW holders are 5.5 times less likely to commit a violent crime.[21]

Fact: "I lobbied against the law in 1993 and 1995 because I thought it would lead to wholesale armed conflict. That hasn't happened. All the horror stories I thought would come to pass didn't happen. No bogeyman. I think it's worked out well, and that says good things about the citizens who have permits. I'm a convert."[22]

Fact: "It has impressed me how remarkably responsible the permit holders have been."[23]

Myth: People do not need concealable weapons

Fact: In 80% of gun defenses, the defender used a concealable handgun. A quarter of the gun defenses occurred in places away from the defender's home.[24]

Fact: 77% of all violent crime occurs in public places.[25] This makes concealed carry necessary for almost all self-defense needs. But due to onerous laws forbidding concealed carry, only 26.8% of defensive gun uses occurred away from home.[26]

Fact: Often, small weapons that are capable of being concealed are the only ones usable by people of small stature or with physical disabilities.

Fact: The average citizen doesn't need a Sport Utility Vehicle, but driving one is arguably safer than driving other vehicles. Similarly, carrying a concealable gun makes the owner — and his or her community — safer by providing protection not otherwise available.

Fact: 56% of Americans say more concealed weapons would make the country safer.[27] Millions of Americans have concealed carry permits, and this doesn't include people who carry in states that do not require permits.

Myth: CCWs will lead to mass public shootings

Fact: Multiple victim public shootings drop in states that pass shall-issue CCW legislation.[28]

Fact: Of all the alternatives to preventing mass public shootings, police officers believe that civilian concealed carry is the most effective. "[29]

Fact: CCW holders have prevented or curtailed mass public shootings – Pearl, Mississippi (Pearl Junior High School), Edinboro, Pennsylvania (Parker Middle School), Winnemucca, Nevada (Players Bar and Grill), and Colorado Springs, Colorado (New Life Church).

Myth: Police and prosecutors are against concealed carrying by citizens

Fact: In a survey of 15,000 officers, 91% said concealed carry should be permitted citizens "without question and without further restrictions."[30]

Fact: 66% of police chiefs believe that citizens carrying concealed firearms reduce rates of violent crime.[31]

Fact: "All the horror stories I thought would come to pass didn't happen ...I think it's worked out well, and that says good things about the citizens who have permits. I'm a convert."[32]

Fact: "I ... [felt] that such legislation present[ed] a clear and present danger to law-abiding citizens by placing more handguns on our streets. Boy was I wrong. Our experience in Harris County, and indeed statewide, has proven my fears absolutely groundless."[33]

Murder and Injuries in Multiple Victim Public Shootings

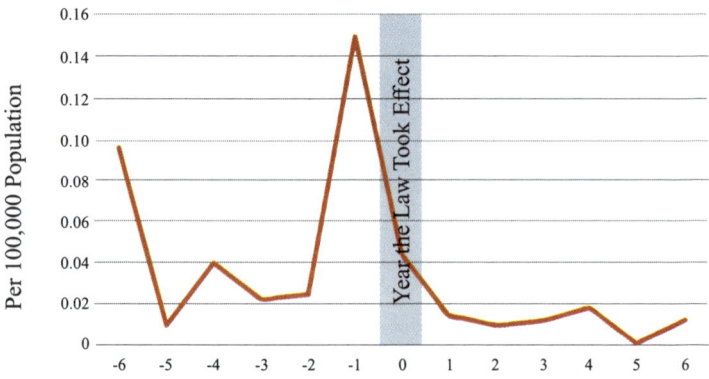

Year Before/After CCWs Were Available

Fact: "Virginia has not turned into Dodge City. We have not seen a problem."[34]

Fact: "The concerns I had – with more guns on the street, folks may be more apt to square off against one another with weapons – we haven't experienced that."[35]

Fact: "… to the best of my knowledge, we have not had an issue. I had expected there would be a lot more problems … But it has actually worked out."[36]

Fact: "Coming from California [where he was on the Los Angeles police force for 28 years], where it takes an act of Congress to get a concealed weapon permit, I got to Maine, where they give out lots of carrying concealed weapon permits, and I had a stack of CCW permits I was denying; that was my orientation. I changed my orientation real quick. Maine is one of the safest places in America. Clearly, suspects knew that good Americans were armed."[37]

Fact: Explain this to the Law Enforcement Alliance of America, the Second Amendment Police Department, and the Law Enforcement for the Preservation of the Second

Amendment, all of whom support shall-issue concealed carry law.

1. Florida Department of Justice, 1998
2. *An examination of the effects of concealed weapons laws and assault weapons bans on state-level murder rates*, Applied Economics Letters, Vol 21, No. 4
3. *Shall issue: the new wave of concealed handgun permit laws,* Cramer C and Kopel D. Golden CO: Independence Institute Issue Paper. October 17, 1994
4. Some criminologists believe measuring first year change is shortsighted as it takes more than a year for permits to be issued, reach critical quantities, and for the criminally minded to recognize the new situation and avoid violent confrontations.
5. Bureau of Justice Statistics, online database, reviewing Texas and U.S. violent crime from 1995-2001.
6. FBI, Uniform Crime Reports, 2004 - excludes Hawaii and Rhode Island - small populations and geographic isolation create other determinants to violent crime.
7. Federal legislation created a national "gun-free schools" policy, effective in 1996. Some criminologists maintain this created a new dynamic, encouraging mass murder on campus. Thus, after 1995 it is increasingly difficult to make comparisons based on the effects of CCWs and mass shootings.
8. *Multiple Victim Public Shootings, Bombings, and Right-to-Carry Concealed Handgun Laws: Contrasting Private and Public Law Enforcement*, John Lott and William Landes, Law School of the University of Chicago, Law & Economics Working Paper No. 73
9. *Crime, Deterrence, and Right-to-Carry Concealed Handguns*, Lott, John R., and Mustard, David B. J. of Legal Studies, vol.26, n.1, pp.1-68 (Jan. 1997): This study involved county level crime statistics from *all* 3,054 counties in the U.S., from 1977 through 1992. During this time ten states adopted right-to-carry laws. It is estimated that if all states had adopted right-to-carry laws, in 1992 the US would have avoided 1,400 murders, 4,200 rapes, 12,000 robberies, 60,000 aggravated assaults – and saved over $5,000,000,000 in victim expenses.
10. *Law Enforcement Officers Killed by Concealed Handgun Permit Holders*, VPC, December 13, 2009
11. Texas Department of Public Safety and the U.S. Census Bureau, reported in San Antonio Express-News, September, 2000
12. *An Analysis of the Arrest Rate of Texas Concealed Carry Handgun*

License Holders as Compared to the Arrest Rate of the Entire Texas Population, William E. Sturdevant, PE, September 11, 1999

13. Nina Butts, Texans Against Gun Violence, Dallas Morning News, August 10, 2000

14. John Holmes, Harris County [Houston, TX] District Attorney, *In Session: Handgun Law's First Year Belies Fears of 'Blood in the Streets,''* Texas Lawyer, December 9, 1996

15. *Concealed Weapons/Firearms License Statistical Report*, Florida Department of State, 1998 – Florida Game and Fresh Water Fish Commission, December 1998

16. State-by-state tally from licensing records conducted by Crime Prevention Research Center

17. *Gun Crimes Drop at Virginia Bars and Restaurants*, Richmond Times-Dispatch, August 14, 2011, reporting data from the Virginia State Police

18. *Basis for Revocation or Suspension of Texas Concealed*, Texas Department of Public Safety, December 1, 1998

19. Texas Department of Corrections data, 1996-2000, compiled by the Texas State Rifle Association, www.tsra.com[/ref] The

20. These are year 2000 records. As of 2014, the number of Texas concealed carry license holders was 825,957.

21. *An Analysis of the Arrest Rate of Texas Concealed Handgun License Holders as Compared to The Arrest Rate of the Entire Texas Population*, William E. Sturdevant, PE, September 11, 1999

22. Glenn White, President of the Dallas Police Association, Dallas Morning News, December 23, 1997

23. Colonel James Wilson, Director Texas Department of Public Safety, Dallas Morning News, June 11, 1996

24. *Armed Resistance to Crime: The Prevalence and Nature of Self-Defense with a Gun*, by Gary Kleck and Marc Gertz, in The Journal of Criminal Law & Criminology, Northwestern University School of Law, Volume 86, Number 1, Fall, 1995

25. *Criminal Victimization in the United States*, U.S. Bureau of Justice Statistics, 1993

26. Kleck and Gertz, National Self Defense Survey, 1995

27. *Majority Say More Concealed Weapons Would Make U.S. Safer*, Gallup Poll, October, 2015

28. *Multiple Victim Public Shootings, Bombings, and Right-to-Carry Concealed Handgun Laws: Contrasting Private and Public Law Enforcement,* Lott John R., Landes William M.; University of Chicago — Covers years 1977 to 1995

29. *Gun Policy & Law Enforcement*, PoliceOne, March 2013

30. *Gun Policy & Law Enforcement*, PoliceOne, arch 2013

31. National Association of Chiefs of Police, 17th Annual National Survey

of Police Chiefs & Sheriffs, 2005

32. Glenn White, president, Dallas Police Association, Dallas Morning News, December 23, 1997

33. John B. Holmes, Harris County Texas district attorney, Dallas Morning News, December 23, 1997

34. Jerry Kilgore, Virginia Public Safety Secretary, Fredricksburg Freelance Star, February 2, 1996

35. Chief Dennis Nowicki, Charlotte-Mecklenburg North Carolina Police, News and Observer, November 24, 1997

36. Lt. William Burgess of the Calhoun County (Michigan) Sheriff Department, Battle Creek Enquirer, January 28, 2005

37. Detroit Police Chief James Craig, *Detroit police chief: Legal gun owners can deter crime,* The Detroit News, January 3, 2014

Assault Weapons

"Assault weapon" is an invented term. In the firearm lexicon, there is no such thing as an "assault weapon."[1] The closest relative is the "assault rifle," which is a machine gun or "select fire" rifle that shoots rifle cartridges.[2] In most cases, "assault weapons" are functionally identical though less powerful than hunting rifles, but they are *cosmetically* similar to military guns.

Myth: Assault weapons are a serious problem in the U.S.

Fact: In 1994, before the Federal "assault weapons ban," you were eleven (11) times more likely to be beaten to death than to be killed by an "assault weapon."[3]

Fact: In the first 7 years since the ban was lifted, murders declined 43%, violent crime 43%, rapes 27% and robberies 49%.[4]

Fact: Nationally, "assault weapons" were used in 1.4% of crimes involving firearms and 0.25% of all violent crime before the enactment of any national or state "assault weapons" ban. In many major urban areas (San Antonio, Mobile, Nashville, etc.) and some entire states (Maryland, New Jersey, etc.) the rate is less than 0.1%.[5]

Fact: Even weapons misclassified as "assault weapons" (common in the former Federal and California "assault weapons" confiscations) are used in less than 1% of all homicides.[6]

Fact: Only 1.4% of recovered crime weapons are models covered under the 1994 "assault weapons" ban.[7]

Fact: In Virginia, no surveyed inmates had carried an "assault weapon" during the commission of their last crime, despite 20% admitting that they had previously owned such weapons.[8]

Fact: Police reports show that "assault weapons" are a non-problem: For California:

- Los Angeles: In 1998, of 538 documented gun incidents, only one (0.2%) involved an "assault weapon."

- San Francisco: In 1998, only 2.2% of confiscated weapons were "assault weapons."

- San Diego: Between 1988 and 1990, only 0.3% of confiscated weapons were "assault weapons."

- "I surveyed the firearms used in violent crimes...assault-type firearms were the least of our worries."[9]

For the rest of the nation:

- Between 1980 and 1994, only 2% of confiscated guns were "assault weapons."[10]

- Fewer than 2% of criminals that commit violent crimes used "assault weapons."[11]

Fact: Most "assault weapons" have no more firepower or killing capacity than the average hunting rifle and "play a small role in overall violent crime."[12]

Fact: Even the government agrees. "... the weapons banned by this legislation [1994 Federal Assault Weapons ban - since repealed] were used only rarely in gun crimes."[13]

Myth: Assault weapons are used in mass public shootings

Fact: A decade long study, covering 84 mass public shootings, found that pistols were used 60% of the time. Rifles were used 27%.[14] But that is *all* types of rifles, and so-called "assault weapons" (such as the AR-15 or civilian versions of the AK-47) are a subset of these.

Myth: Every 48 hours, an assault rifle is traced to crime in Maryland

Fact: This claim by Cease Fire Maryland includes firearms never used in crimes. Some examples of firearms traced include:

- 47 firearms found at a private residence of a person who passed-away from natural causes, and which were never used in any crime.
- Firearms temporarily taken from owners under court Emergency Evaluation Petitions (the firearms were not used in crimes, but the judge wanted them confiscated until other issues are resolved).

Fact: This claim lacks perspective. During the same time period, there were 163,101 violent crimes reported in Maryland. Even if the Cease Fire Maryland data was correct, they have connected assault rifles to just 0.4% of violent crimes during the same period.

Myth: One out of five police officers killed are killed with assault weapons[15]

Fact: This "study" included firearms not on the former Federal "assault weapons" list. By including various legal firearms[16] the report inflated the statistics nearly 100%.

Fact: Only 1% of police officers murdered were killed using "assault weapons." They were twice as likely to be killed with their own handgun.[17]

Fact: One 2006 federal government study found *zero* "assault weapons" were used to kill police officers.[18]

Fact: Police don't think it is a major problem, with 91% saying an assault weapons ban would have either no effect or a negative effect on violent crime.[19]

Myth: Assault weapons are favored by criminals

Fact: Only 6% of criminals use anything that is classified (even incorrectly) as an "assault weapon,"[20] and fewer than 2.5% of criminal claimed to use these firearms when committing crimes.[21]

Fact: Criminals are over five times more likely to carry single shot handguns as they are to carry "assault weapons."[22]

Fact: "Assault rifles have never been an issue in law enforcement. I have been on this job for 25 years and I haven't seen a drug dealer carry one. They are not used in crimes, they are not used against police officers."[23]

Fact: "Since police started keeping statistics, we now know that 'assault weapons' are/were used in an underwhelming 0.026 of 1% of crimes in New Jersey. This means that my officers are more likely to confront an escaped tiger from the local zoo than to confront an assault rifle in the hands of a drug-crazed killer on the streets."[24]

Thoughts: "Assault weapons" are large and unwieldy. Even misclassified handguns tend to be bigger than practical for concealed carry. Criminals (who, incidentally, disregard concealed carry laws) are unlikely to carry "assault weapons" and instead carry handguns, which are more easily concealed.

Myth: Assault weapons can be easily converted to machine guns

Fact: Firearms that can be "readily converted" are already prohibited by law.[25]

Fact: None of the firearms on the list of banned weapons can be readily converted.[26]

Fact: Only 0.15% of over 4,000 weapons confiscated in Los Angeles in one year were converted, and only 0.3% had any evidence of an attempt to convert.[27]

Myth: Assault weapons are used in 16% of homicides

Fact: This figure was concocted to promote an "assault weapons" bill in New York. Their classification scheme included most firearms sold in the U.S. since 1987 (centerfire rifles, shotguns holding more than six cartridges, and handguns holding more than 10 rounds). By misclassifying most firearms as "assault weapons," they expanded the scope of a non-problem.

Myth: The 1994 (former) Federal Assault Weapons Ban was effective

Fact: Murder rates were 19.3% higher when the Federal assault weapons ban was in force.[28]

Fact: " ... we cannot clearly credit the ban with any of the nation's recent drop in gun violence."[29]

Fact: The ban covered only 1.39% of the models of firearms on the market, so the ban's effectiveness is automatically limited.

Fact: "The ban has failed to reduce the average number of victims per gun murder incident or multiple gunshot wound victims."[30]

Fact: "The public safety benefits of the 1994 ban have not yet been demonstrated."[31]

Fact: "The ban triggered speculative price increases and ramped-up production of the banned firearms ... prior to the law's implementation,"[32] and thus increased the total supply over the following decade.

Fact: The Brady Campaign claims that "After the 1994 ban, there were 18% fewer 'assault weapons' traced to crime in the first eight months of 1995 than were traced in the same period in 1994." However, they failed to note (and these are mentioned in the NIJ study) that:

1. "Assault weapons" traces were minimal before the ban (due to their infrequent use in crimes), so an 18% change enters the realm of statistical irrelevancy.

2. Fewer "assault weapons" were available to criminals because collectors bought-up the available supply before the ban.

Myth: States need to ban assault weapons

Fact: State assault weapons bans "did not significantly affect murder rates" in a study covering 1980-2009. [33]

Myth: Assault weapons have only one purpose, to kill large numbers of people

Fact: Of the millions of these firearms currently in civilian hands, they are routinely used for:

- Small game hunting (especially hog hunting in thick southern brush)
- Sports competitions such as "three gun shoots"
- Self-defense, both at home and during civil disorder situations such as the Rodney King riots in L.A. and Hurricane Katrina

Myth: Nobody needs an assault weapon

Fact: Their light weight and durability make them suitable for many types of hunting and are especially favored for wild boar hunting.

Fact: Their lighter recoil combined with light weight make them the preferred rifle with people of small stature or limited strength.

Fact: Recall the 1992 Rodney King riots in the anti-gun city of Los Angeles. Every major news network carried footage of Korean store owners sitting on the roofs of their stores, armed with "assault weapons."[34] Those were the stores that did *not* get burned to the ground, and those were the people that were *not* dragged into the street and beaten by rioters. "You can't get around the image of people shooting at people to protect their stores and it working. This is damaging to the [gun control] movement."[35]

Fact: There are many reasons people prefer to use these firearms:

- They are easy to operate
- They are very reliable in outdoor conditions (backpacking, hunting, etc.)
- They are accurate
- They are good for recreational and competitive target shooting
- They have value in many self-defense situations

Fact: There are many sports in which these firearms are required:

- Many hunters use these firearms (especially for wild boar hunting in the south)
- Three-gun target matches
- Camp Perry competitions, especially the Service Rifle events
- DCM/CMP competitions
- Bodyguard simulations

Fact: Ours is a Bill of *Rights*, not a Bill of *Needs*.

1. It is worth noting that there are numerous different 'legal' definitions of "assault weapons". A report from the Legal Community Against Violence showed no fewer than eight jurisdictions, anywhere from 19 to 75 banned firearms, six differing generic classification schemes and several legal systems for banning more firearms without specific legislative action. In other words, an "assault weapon" is whatever a politician deems it to be.

2. *Small Arms Identification and Operations Guide*, U.S. Department of Defense. The exact statement from their manual is "short, compact, **select-fire** weapons that fires a cartridge intermediate in power between submachine gun and rifle cartridges."

3. Based on death rates reported by CDC and FBI Uniform Crime Statistics and estimating from state-level reporting on the percent of crimes involving types of firearms

4. FBI Uniform Crime Statistics, Uniform Crime Reporting Statistics - UCR Data Online, 1995-2012

5. *Targeting Guns*, Gary Kleck, Aldine Transaction, 1997, compilation of 48 metropolitan police departments from 1980-1994

6. Based on state-level reporting from various states in 1993 during debates concerning the bill.

7. From statewide recovery report from Connecticut (1988-1993) and Pennsylvania (1989-1994)

8. Criminal Justice Research Center, Department of Criminal Justice Services, 1994

9. S.C. Helsley, Assistant Director DOJ Investigation and Enforcement Branch, California, October 31, 1988

10. *Targeting Guns*, Gary Kleck, Aldine Transaction, 1997, compilation of 48 metropolitan police departments from 1980-1994

11. *Targeting Guns*, Gary Kleck, Aldine Transaction, 1997, calculated from Bureau of Justice Statistics, assault weapon recovery rates

12. House Panel Issue: Can Gun Ban Work, New York Times. April 7, 1989. P. A-15, quoting Philip McGuire, Handgun Control, Inc.,

13. Impacts of the 1994 Assault Weapons Ban: 1994-96, National Institute of Justice, March 1999

14. *United States Active Shooter Events from 2000 to 2010: Training and Equipment Implications*, Advanced Law Enforcement Rapid Response Training (ALERRT), Texas State University, 2013

15. This claim was made by the anti-gun Violence Policy Center in their 2003 report titled Officer Down

16. The study included legal models of the SKS, Ruger Mini-14, and M1-Carbine, which were all in circulation before the federal "assault weapons" ban and which were excluded from the ban.

17. Law Enforcement Officers Killed and Assaulted, FBI, 1994

18. *Violent Encounters: A Study of Felonious Assaults on Our Nation's Law*

Enforcement Officers, U.S. Department of Justice, August 2006

19. Gun Policy & Law Enforcement, PoliceOne, March 2013

20. Firearm Use by Offenders, Bureau of Justice Statistics, November 2001

21. Firearm Use by Offenders, Bureau of Justice Statistics, November 2001

22. Firearm Use by Offenders, Bureau of Justice Statistics, November 2001

23. Deputy Chief of Police Joseph Constance, Trenton, NJ, testimony - Senate Judiciary Committee in Aug 1993

24. Deputy Chief of Police Joseph Constance, Trenton, NJ, testimony - Senate Judiciary Committee in Aug 1993

25. U.S. Code title 26, subtitle E, Chapter 53, subchapter B, part 1, section 5845

26. BATF test as reported in the New York Times, April 3, 1989

27. Congressional testimony, Jimmy Trahin, Los Angeles Detective, Subcommittee on the Constitution of the Committee on the Judiciary, May 5, 1989, 101st Congress, 1st Session, Washington, DC, US Government Printing Office, May 5, 1989, p. 379

28. *An examination of the effects of concealed weapons laws and assault weapons bans on state-level murder rates*, Applied Economics Letters, Vol 21, No. 4

29. An Updated Assessment of the Federal Assault Weapons Ban: Impacts on Gun Markets and Gun Violence, 1994-2003, National Institute of Justice, June 2004

30. Impacts of the 1994 Assault Weapons Ban: 1994-96, National Institute of Justice, March 1999

31. Impacts of the 1994 Assault Weapons Ban: 1994-96, National Institute of Justice, March 1999

32. Impacts of the 1994 Assault Weapons Ban: 1994-96, National Institute of Justice, March 1999

33. *An examination of the effects of concealed weapons laws and assault weapons bans on state-level murder rates*, Applied Economics Letters, Vol 21, No. 4

34. Washington Post, May 2, 1992

35. Josh Sugarmann, executive director of the Violence Policy Center, Washington Post, May 18, 1993

Guns and Crime Prevention

Myth: **Private ownership of guns is not effective in preventing crime**

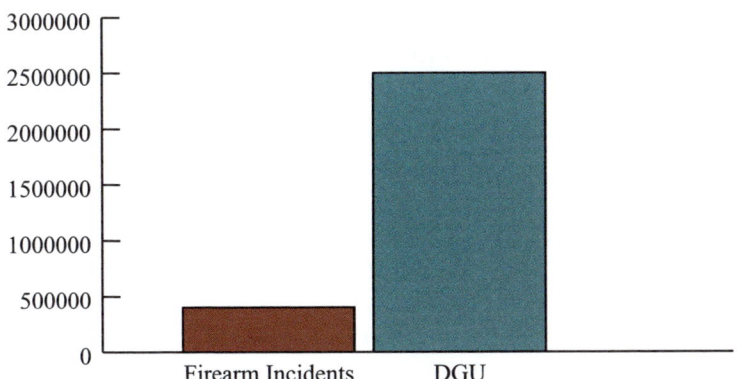

Defensive Gun Use (DGU) v. Firearm Violent Crime

Fact: Every year, people in the United States use guns to defend themselves against criminals an estimated 2,500,000 times – more than 6,500 people a day, or once every 13 seconds.[1] Of these instances, 15.7% of the people using firearms defensively stated that they "almost certainly" saved their lives by doing so.

Fact: Even the government's estimate, which has a major methodology problem,[2] estimates people defend themselves 235,700 times each year with guns. [3]

Fact: The number of times per year an American uses a firearm to deter a home invasion alone is 498,000.[4]

Fact: In 83.5% (2,087,500) of these successful gun defenses, the attacker either threatened or used force first, proving that guns are very well suited for self-defense.

Fact: The rate of defensive gun use (DGU) is six times that of criminal gun use.[5]

Fact: Of the 2,500,000 times citizens use guns to defend themselves, 92% merely brandish their gun or fire a warning shot to scare off their attackers.[6]

Fact: In most of the remaining 8% of defensive gun uses, a citizen never wounds his or her attacker (they fire warning shots), and in less than one in a thousand instances is the attacker killed.[7]

Fact: In one local review of firearm homicide, more than 12% were civilian legal defensive homicides.[8]

Fact: For every accidental death (802), suicide (16,869) or homicide (11,348)[9] with a firearm (29,019), 13 lives (390,000)[10] are preserved through defensive use.

Fact: When using guns in self-defense, 91.1% of the time, not a single shot is fired.[11]

Fact: After the implementation of Canada's 1977 gun controls prohibiting handgun possession for protection, the "breaking and entering" crime rate rose 25%, surpassing the American rate.[12]

Myth: Only police should have guns

Fact: "Most criminals are more worried about meeting an armed victim than they are about running into the police."[13]

Fact: For kids in schools, police end such attacks only 27% of the time.[14]

Fact: 11% of police shootings kill an innocent person — about 2% of shootings by citizens kill an innocent person.[15]

Fact: Police have trouble keeping their own guns. Hundreds of firearms are missing from the FBI and 449 of them have been involved in crimes.[16]

Fact: People who saw the helplessness of the L.A. Police Department during the 1992 King Riots or the looting and violence in New Orleans after hurricane Katrina know that citizens need guns to defend themselves.

Fact: "In actual shootings, citizens do far better than law enforcement on hit potential. They hit their targets and they don't hit other people. I wish I could say the same for cops. We train more, they do better."[17]

Myth: You are more likely to be injured or killed using a gun for self-defense

Fact: You are far more likely to survive violent assault if you defend yourself with a gun.[18]

Myth: Guns are not effective in preventing crime against women

Fact: Of the 2,500,000 annual self-defense cases using guns, more than 7.7% (192,500) are by women defending themselves against sexual abuse.

Fact: When a woman was armed with a gun or knife, only 3% of rape attacks were completed, compared to 32% when the woman was unarmed.[19]

Reported Rape Rates 1995-2003 (per 100,000 population)			
	1995	2003	% Change
Australia	72.5	91.7	+26.5
United Kingdom	43.3	69.2	+59.8
United States	37.1	32.1	-13.5

Fact: The probability of serious injury from an attack is 2.5 times greater for women offering no resistance than for women resisting with guns. Men also benefit from using guns, but the benefits are smaller: Men are 1.4 times more likely to receive a serious injury.[20]

Injury Rate by Self Protection Mode

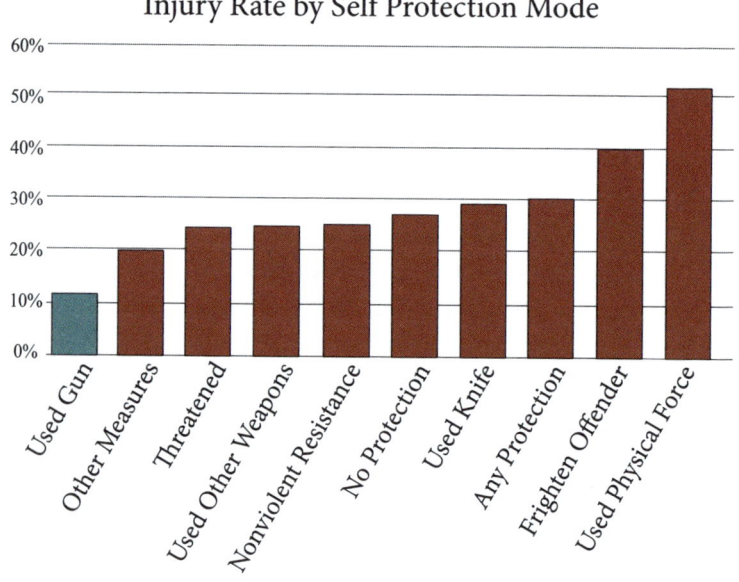

Fact: 28.5% of women have one or more guns in the house.[21]

Fact: 41.7% of women either own or have convenient access to guns.[22]

Fact: In 1966, the city of Orlando responded to a wave of sexual assaults by offering firearms training classes to women. Rapes dropped by nearly 90% the following year.

Fact: Firearm availability appears to be particularly useful in avoiding rape. The United Kingdom virtually banned handgun ownership. During the same period handgun ownership in the United States steadily rose. Yet the rate of rape decreased in the United States and skyrocketed in the other countries, as shown in the table.

Fact: More Americans believe having a gun in the home makes them safer. This belief grows every year the survey is taken.[23]

Fact: Arthur Kellerman, a researcher whose work is often cited by gun control groups, said "If you've got to resist, your chances of being hurt are less the more lethal your weapon. If that were my wife, would I want her to have a .38 Special in her hand? Yeah."[24]

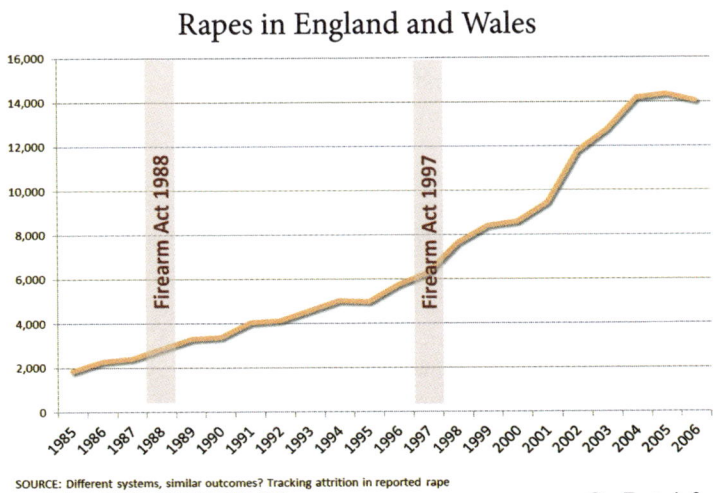

Rapes in England and Wales

SOURCE: Different systems, similar outcomes? Tracking attrition in reported rape cases in eleven countries., J. Lovett, L. Kelley, 2009

www.GunFacts.info

1. Journal of Criminal Law and Criminology, Kleck and Gertz, Fall 1995
2. This ongoing victimization survey involved people from the government personally interviewing victims in person. Some criminologists believe this induces self-reporting biases (e.g., people don't like to tell the government they own a gun). Thus, this low number from the National Crime Victimization Survey is considered to be an outlier and not reliable.
3. *Firearm Violence, 1993-2011,* Bureau of Justice Statistics, May 2013
4. Estimating intruder-related firearm retrievals in U.S. households, 1994. Robin M. Ikeda, Violence and Victims, Winter 1997
5. Crime statistics: Bureau of Justice Statistics - National Crime Victimization Survey (2005). DGU statistics: Targeting Guns, Kleck (average of 15 major surveys where DGUs were reported)
6. Targeting Guns, Gary Kleck, Aldine de Gruyter, 1997, from the National Self-Defense Survey
7. Targeting Guns, Gary Kleck, Aldine de Gruyter, 1997, from the National Self-Defense Survey
8. Death by Gun: One Year Later, Time Magazine, May 14, 1990
9. Unintentional Firearm Deaths, 2001, U.S. Centers for Disease Control and Prevention, National Center for Injury Prevention and Control
10. Targeting Guns, Gary Kleck, Aldine de Gruyter, 1997
11. National Crime Victimization Survey, 2000
12. Residential Burglary: A Comparison of the United States, Canada and England and Wales, Pat Mayhew, National Institute of Justice., Wash., D.C., 1987
13. Armed and Considered Dangerous: A Survey of Felons and Their Firearms, Wright and Rossi, 1986
14. *Implications for the Prevention of School Attacks,* United States Secret Service and United States Department of Education, 2002
15. Shall issue: the new wave of concealed handgun permit laws, Clayton Cramer, David Kopel, Independence Institute Issue Paper. October 17, 1994
16. ABC News, July 17, 2001
17. Sheriff Greg White, Cole County, Missouri, Guns to be allowed on campus? KRCG News, July 31, 2009
18. The Value of Civilian Handgun Possession as a Deterrent to Crime or a Defense Against Crime, Don B. Kates, 1991 American Journal of Criminal Law
19. Law Enforcement Assistance Administration, Rape Victimization in 26 American Cities, U.S. Department of Justice, 1979
20. National Crime Victimization Survey, Department of Justice
21. 2001 National Gun Policy Survey of the National Opinion Research Center: Research Findings, Smith, T, National Opinion Research Center, University of Chicago, December 2001.

22. 2001 National Gun Policy Survey of the National Opinion Research Center: Research Findings, Smith, T, National Opinion Research Center, University of Chicago, December 2001.
23. Americans by Slight Margin Say Gun in the Home Makes It Safer, Gallup Poll, October 20, 2006
24. Gun Crazy, S.F. Examiner, April 3, 1994

Crime and Guns

Basic to the debates on gun control is the fact that most violent crime is committed by repeat offenders. Dealing with recidivism is key to solving violence.

- 71% of gunshot victims had previous arrest records.
- 64% had been convicted of a crime.
- Each had an average of 11 prior arrests.[1,2]
- 63% of victims had criminal histories and 73% of that group knew their assailant (twice as often as victims without criminal histories).[3]
- 74% of homicides during the commission of a felony involve guns.[4]

Most gun violence is between criminals. This should be the public policy focus.

Myth: Criminals buy guns at gun stores and gun shows

Fact: One study [5]of adult offenders living in Chicago or nearby determined that criminals obtain most of their guns through their social network and personal connections. Rarely is the proximate source either direct purchase from a gun store, or even theft. This agrees with other, broader studies of incarcerated felons.

Fact: Another city-wide study,[6] this one in Pittsburgh, showed that 80% of people illegally carrying guns were prohibited from possessing guns, and that a minimum of 30% of the guns were stolen.

Fact: Other common arrangements include sharing guns and holding guns for others.[7]

Myth: Guns are not a good deterrent to crime

Fact: Every year 400,000 life-threatening violent crimes are prevented using firearms.

Fact: 60% of convicted felons admitted that they avoided committing crimes when they knew the victim was armed. 40% of convicted felons admitted that they avoided committing crimes when they thought the victim might be armed.[8]

Fact: Guns prevent an estimated 2.5 million crimes a year or 6,849 every day.[9] Most often, the gun is never fired and no blood (including the criminal's) is shed.

Fact: Property-crime rates are dropping (especially burglaries). The chart shows the legal handgun supply in America (mainly in civilian hands) relative to the property-crime rate.[10]

Fact: Felons report that they avoid entering houses where people are at home because they fear being shot.[11]

Fact: 59% of the burglaries in Britain, which has tough gun control laws, are "hot burglaries"[12] which are burglaries committed while the home is occupied by the owner/renter. By contrast, the U.S., with more lenient gun control laws, has a "hot burglary" rate of only 13%.[13]

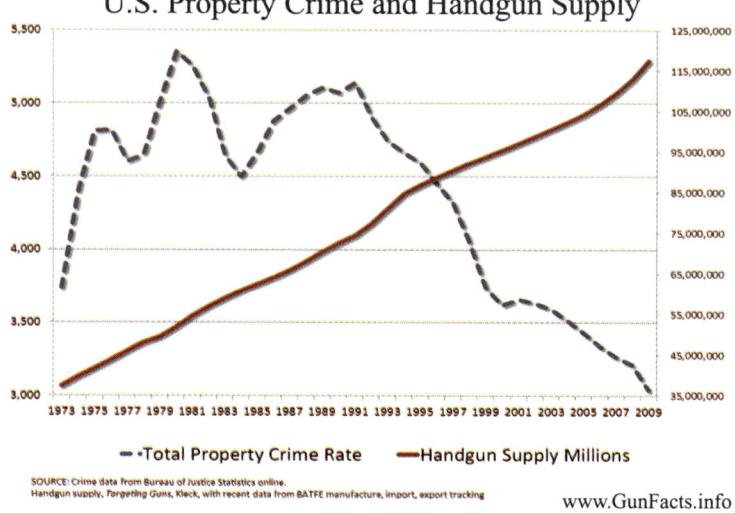

U.S. Property Crime and Handgun Supply

- - Total Property Crime Rate ——Handgun Supply Millions

SOURCE: Crime data from Bureau of Justice Statistics online.
Handgun supply, *Targeting Guns*, Kleck, with recent data from BATFE manufacture, import, export tracking

www.GunFacts.info

Fact: Washington DC has essentially banned gun ownership since 1976[14] and has a murder rate of 56.9 per 100,000. Across the river in Arlington, Virginia, gun ownership is less restricted. There, the murder rate is just 1.6 per 100,000, less than three percent of the Washington, DC rate.[15]

Fact: 26% of all retail businesses report keeping a gun on the premises for crime control.[16]

Fact: In 1982, Kennesaw, GA, passed a law requiring heads of households to keep at least one firearm in the house. The residential burglary rate dropped 89% the following year.[17]

Fact: A survey of felons revealed the following:[18]

- 74% of felons agreed that, "One reason burglars avoid houses when people are at home is that they fear being shot during the crime."

- 57% of felons polled agreed, "Criminals are more worried about meeting an armed victim than they are about running into the police."

SAF Debate Book

Myth: Private guns are used to commit violent crimes

Fact: 90% of all violent crimes in the U.S. do not involve firearms of any type.[19]

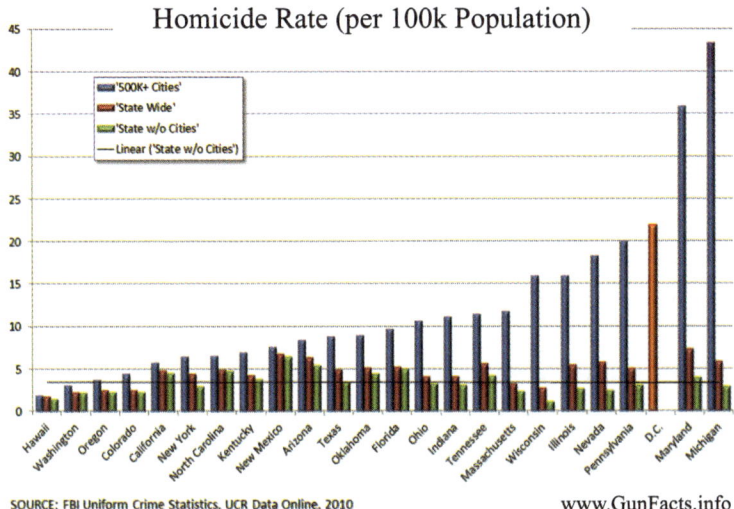

Homicide Rate (per 100k Population)

Legend:
- '500K+ Cities'
- 'State Wide'
- 'State w/o Cities'
- Linear ('State w/o Cities')

SOURCE: FBI Uniform Crime Statistics, UCR Data Online, 2010   www.GunFacts.info

Fact: Even in crimes where the offender possessed a gun during the commission of the crime, 83% did not use or threaten to use the gun.[20]

Fact: Fewer than 1% of firearms will ever be used in the commission of a crime.[21]

Fact: Two-thirds of the people who die each year from gunfire are criminals being shot by other criminals.[22]

Fact: Cincinnati's review of their gang problem revealed that 74% of homicides were committed by less than 1% of the population.[23]

Fact: 92% of gang murders are committed with guns.[24] Gangs are responsible for between 48% and 90% of all violent crimes.[25]

Fact: Most gun crimes are gang related, and as such are big-city issues. In fact, if mayors in larger cities were more diligent about controlling gang warfare, state and nationwide gun violence rates would fall dramatically.

Myth: 40% of Americans have been or personally know a gun violence victim

Fact: This data was from an unpublished survey conducted by a political research organization. Their own footnote reads "Greenberg Quinlan Rosner Research for the New Venture Fund (Aug. 2011). Note: this is not publicly available data."[26]

Myth: Interstate transportation of guns defeats local gun control

Fact: The BATF reports that the average age of a traced gun is 11 years[27], meaning that most guns moving from state to state were transported when legal owners moved.

Fact: Fewer than 5% of traced guns in California, many of which were not crime guns, came from neighboring Nevada and Arizona.[28]

Myth: High-capacity, semi-automatics are preferred by criminals

Fact: The use of semi-automatic handguns in crimes is slightly lower than the ratio of semi-automatic handguns owned by private citizens. Any increase in style and capacity simply reflects the overall supply of the various types of firearms.[29]

Myth: Banning "Saturday Night Specials" reduces crime

Fact: This was the conclusion of the Johns Hopkins University Center for Gun Policy and Research – and it is wrong. They studied firearm homicide rates from Maryland after passage of a "Saturday Night Special" ban in 1998. It seems the firearm homicide rate has not subsided and remained between 68-94% higher than the national average through 2008.[30]

Fact: Even banning guns does not slow down criminals. In the U.K., where private ownership of firearms is practically forbidden, criminals have and use guns regularly, and even build their own. One enterprising fellow converted 170 starter pistols to functioning firearms and sold them to gangs. Hundreds of such underground gun factories have been established, contributing to a 35% jump in gun violence.[31]

Myth: Criminals prefer "Saturday Night Specials"[32]

Fact: "Saturday Night Specials" were used in fewer than 3% of crimes involving guns.[33]

Fact: Fewer than 2% of all "Saturday Night Specials" made are used in crimes.

Fact: "What was available was the overriding factor in weapon choice [by criminals]."[34]

Myth: Gun shows are supermarkets for criminals

Fact: Only 0.7% of convicts bought their firearms at gun shows. 39.2% obtained them from illegal street dealers.[35]

Fact: Fewer than 1% of "crime guns" were obtained at gun shows.[36] This is a reduction from a 1997 study that found 2% of guns used in criminal offenses were purchased at gun shows.[37]

Fact: The FBI concluded in one study that no firearms acquired at gun shows were used to kill police. "In contrast to media myth, none of the firearms in the study were obtained from gun shows."[38]

Fact: Only 5% of metropolitan police departments believe gun shows are a problem.[39]

Fact: Only 3.5% of youthful offenders reported that they obtained their last handgun at a gun show.[40]

Fact: 93% of guns used in crimes are obtained illegally (i.e., not at gun stores or gun shows).[41]

Fact: At most, 14% of all firearms traced in investigations were purchased at gun shows.[42] But this includes all firearms that the police traced, whether or not they were used in crimes, which overstates the acquisition rate.

Fact: Gun dealers are federally licensed. They are bound to stringent rules for sales that apply equally whether they are selling firearms from a storefront or a gun show.[43]

Fact: Most crime guns are either bought off the street from illegal sources (39.2%) or through straw-man purchases by family members or friends (39.6%).[44]

Myth: All four guns used at Columbine were bought at gun shows

Fact: Each of the guns was either bought through an intermediary or someone who knew they were going to underage buyers. In all cases there was a purposeful criminal activity occurring and the actors knew they were breaking the law.

Myth: 25-50% of the vendors at most gun shows are "unlicensed dealers"

Fact: There is no such thing as an "unlicensed dealer," except for people who buy and sell antique — curio — firearms as a hobby (not a business).

Fact: This 25-50% figure can only be achieved if you include those dealers *not selling guns* at these shows. These non-gun dealers include knife makers, ammunition dealers, accessories dealers, military artifact traders, clothing vendors, bumper-sticker sellers, and hobbyists. In short, *50% of the vendors at shows are not selling firearms at all!*

Myth: Regulation of gun shows would reduce "straw sales"

Fact: The main study that makes this claim had no scientific means for determining what sales at the show were "straw sales." Behaviors that Dr. Wintemute cited as "clear evidence" of a straw purchase were observational only and were more likely instances of more experienced acquaintances helping in a purchase decision. No attempts were made to verify that the sales in question were straw sales.[45]

Myth: Prison isn't the answer to crime control

Fact: Why does crime rise when criminals are released from prison early? Because they are likely to commit more crimes. 67.5% were re-arrested for new felonies or serious misdemeanors within three years. Extrapolating, those released felons killed another 2,282 people.[46]

Fact: 45% of state prisoners were, at the time they committed their offense, under conditional supervision in the community – either on probation or on parole.[47] Keeping violent convicts in prison would reduce violent crimes.

Fact: Homicide convicts serve a little more than half of their original sentences.[48] Given that men tend to be less prone to violent behavior as they age,[49] holding them for their full sentences would probably reduce violence significantly.

Fact: Los Angeles County saw repeat offender and re-arrest rates soar after authorities closed jails and released prisoners early. In less than three years, early release of prisoners in LA resulted in:[50]

- 15,775 rearrested convicts
- 1,443 assault charges[51]
- 518 robbery charges
- 215 sex-offense charges
- 16 murder charges

Fact: In 1991, 13,200 homicides were committed by felons on parole or probation. For comparison sake, this is about half of the 1999 annual gun death totals (keep in mind that gun deaths fell from 1991 to 1999).

Myth: Waiting periods prevent rash crimes and reduce violent crime rates

Fact: The "time-to-crime" of a firearm is about 11 years, making it rare that a newly purchased firearm is used in a crime.[52]

Fact: The national five-day waiting period under the Brady Bill had no impact on murder or robbery. In fact, there was a slight increase in rape and aggravated assault, indicating no effective suppression of certain violent crimes. Thus, for two crime categories, a possible effect was to delay law-abiding citizens from getting a gun for protection. The risks were greatest for crimes against women.[53]

Fact: Comparing homicide rates in 18 states that had waiting periods and background checks before the Brady Bill with rates in the 32 states that had no comparable laws, the difference in change of homicide rates was "insignificant".[54]

Myth: 86% of Americans, 82% of gun owners favor universal background checks

Fact: Those statistics came from a pair of surveys reported by gun control group Mayors Against Illegal Guns, who has been caught stacking survey responses by polling left-of-center mailing lists.

Myth: Gun makers are selling plastic guns that slip through metal detectors

Fact: There is no such thing as a 'plastic gun'. This myth started in 1980[55] when Glock began marketing a handgun with a polymer frame, not the entire firearm. Most of a Glock is metal (83% by weight) and detectable in common metal and x-ray detectors. "[D]espite a relatively common impression to the contrary, there is no current non-metal firearm not reasonably detectable by present technology and methods in use at our airports today, nor to my knowledge, is anyone on the threshold of developing such a firearm."[56] Incidentally, Glocks are one of the favorite handguns of police departments *because it is lightweight, thanks to the polymer frame.*

Myth: Machine guns[57] are favored by criminals

Fact: In the drug-ridden Miami of 1980, fewer than 1% of all gun homicides were with machine guns.[58]

Fact: None of over 2,220 firearms recovered from crime scenes by the Minneapolis police in 1987-89 were machine guns.[59]

Fact: 0.7% of seized guns in Detroit in 1991-92 were machine guns.[60]

Myth: Corrupt dealers sell almost 60 percent of crime guns

Fact: Only 0.5% of the reported traces were for an original purchase of three years or less before the trace was conducted.[61] Thus, 99.5% of retailer sales had left their control long before the gun was traced (and many traces are not for crime guns).

Fact: The average "time to crime", the time between the retail sale of a firearm and its use in a crime, is eleven years. A firearm can change hands and travel far in six years.

1. Richard Lumb, Paul Friday, City of Charlotte Gunshot Study, Department of Criminal Justice, 1994
2. Homicides and Non-Fatal Shootings: A Report on the First 6 Months of

2009, Milwaukee Homicide Review Commission, July 13, 2009

3. Firearm-related Injury Incidents in 1999 – Annual Report, San Francisco Department of Public Health and San Francisco Injury Center, February 2002

4. *Homicide Trends in the United States, 1980-2008*, Bureau of Justice Statistics, November 2011

5. *Sources of guns to dangerous people: What we learn by asking them,* Cook, Parker, Pollack, Preventive Medicine, Volume 79, October 2015

6. *Gaps continue in firearm Surveillance: Evidence from a large U.S. city Bureau of Police,* Fabio, Duell, Creppage, O'Donnell and Laporte, Social Medicine, Vol 1, 2016

7. *Sources of guns to dangerous people: What we learn by asking them,* Cook, Parker, Pollack, Preventive Medicine, Volume 79, October 2015

8. Armed and Considered Dangerous: A Survey of Felons and Their Firearms, James Wright and Peter Rossi, Aldine, 1986

9. Targeting Guns, Dr. Gary Kleck, Criminologist, Florida State University, Aldine, 1997

10. National Crime Victimization Survey, 2000, Bureau of Justice Statistics, BATF estimates on handgun supply

11. Armed and Considered Dangerous: A Survey of Felons and Their Firearms, James Wright and Peter Rossi, Aldine, 1986

12. A "hot burglary" is when the burglar enters a home while the residents are there

13. Dr. Gary Kleck, Criminologist, Florida State University (1997) and Kopel (1992 and 1999)

14. The Supreme Court invalidated the D.C. handgun ban in the Heller case (2008), but the city has made obtaining a handgun very difficult via local legislation

15. Crime in the United States, FBI, 1998

16. Crime Against Small Business, U.S. Small Business Administration, Senate Document No. 91-14, 1969

17. Crime Control Through the Private Use of Armed Force, Dr. Gary Kleck, Social Problems, February 1988

18. The Armed Criminal in America: A Survey of Incarcerated Felons, U.S. Bureau of Justice Statistics Federal Firearms Offenders study, 1997: National Institute of Justice, Research Report, July 1985, Department of Justice

19. Bureau of Alcohol, Tobacco and Firearms, 1998

20. National Crime Victimization Survey, 1994, Bureau of Justice Statistics

21. FBI Uniform Crime Statistics, 1994

22. FBI Uniform Crime Statistics, 1994

23. *Implementation of the Cincinnati Initiative to Reduce Violence (CIRV),* University of Cincinnati Policing Institute, 2008

24. Homicide trends in the United States, Bureau of Justice Statistics, November 2011

25. 2011 National Gang Threat Assessment, FBI, September 2011

26. Preventing Gun Violence Through Effective Messaging, OMP, KNP Communications, 2012

27. BATF report #133664, California Tracing Reports for 2012

28. BATF report #133664, California Tracing Reports for 2012

29. Targeting Guns, Dr. Gary Kleck, Criminologist, Florida State University, Aldine, 1997

30. Injury Mortality Reports 1999-2008, Center for Disease Control, online database

31. Gun crime spreads 'like a cancer' across Britain, The Guardian, Oct 5, 2003

32. "Saturday Night Special" is a term, with racist origin, describing an inexpensive firearm. Part of the origin of the term came from "suicide special", describing an inexpensive handgun purchased specifically for committing suicide. The racist origins are too detestable to repeat here.

33. FBI Uniform Crime Statistics, 1994

34. Violent Encounters: A Study of Felonious Assaults on Our Nation's Law Enforcement Officers, U.S. Department of Justice, August 2006

35. Firearm Use by Offenders, Bureau of Justice Statistics, February 2002

36. Violent Encounters: A Study of Felonious Assaults on Our Nation's Law Enforcement Officers, U.S. Department of Justice, August 2006

37. Homicide in Eight U.S. Cities, National Institute of Justice, December 1997

38. Violent Encounters: A Study of Felonious Assaults on Our Nation's Law Enforcement Officers, U.S. Department of Justice, August 2006

39. On the Front Line: Making Gun Interdiction Work, Center to Prevent Handgun Violence, February 1998, survey of 37 police departments in large cities

40. Patterns in Gun Acquisition and Use by Youthful Offenders in Michigan, Timothy S. Bynum, Todd G. Beitzel, Tracy A. O'Connell & Sean P. Varano, 1999

41. BATF, 1999

42. BATF, June 2000, covers only July 1996 through December 1998

43. BATF, 2000

44. Firearm use by Offenders, Bureau of Justice Statistics, November 2001

45. Gun shows across a multistate American gun market, Dr. GJ Wintemute, British Medical Journal, 2007

46. Reentry Trends in the U.S., Recidivism, Department of Justice, 1999

47. US Bureau of Justice Statistics, 1991

48. Firearm Use by Offenders, Bureau of Justice Statistics, November, 2001

49. Homicide rates peak in the 18-24-year-old group, Bureau of Justice Statistics, online database

50. Releasing Inmates Early Has a Costly Human Toll, Los Angeles Times, May 14, 2006

51. Keep in mind these are just charges. Each arrested convict may have committed multiple crimes.

52. Bureau of Alcohol, Tobacco and Firearms as reported by Time Magazine, July 12, 2002

53. Dr. John Lott Jr., University of Chicago School of Law, 1997

54. Dr. Jens Ludwig, Dr. Philip J. Cook, Journal of the American Medical Association, August 2000

55. Heckler and Koch made a polymer framed firearm earlier, in 1968, but the myth seems to have erupted after Glock began promoting theirs to police departments.

56. Billie Vincent, FAA Director of Civil Aviation Security, House Subcommittee on Crime, May 15, 1986

57. In this myth, "machine gun" represents "fully automatic" firearms, ones that fire bullets as long as the trigger is pulled

58. Miami Herald, August 23, 1984, based on figures from Dr. Joseph Davis, Dade County medical examiner

59. 1994, Minnesota Medical Association Firearm Injury Prevention Task Force

60. J. Gayle Mericle, 1989, Unpublished report of the Metropolitan Area Narcotics Squad, Will and Grundy Counties

61. Following the Gun: Enforcing Federal Law Against Firearms Traffickers, BATF, 2000

Children and Guns

Myth: There have been 96 school shootings since Sandy Hook

Fact: This analysis of news reports was created by the gun control group Everytown. This study included:

- College campuses (47% of cases)
- Suicides attempts (18%)
- Cases where nobody was hurt (27%)

Some other analysts note that many of the cases are unrelated to school activity or actually occurred near campus, not on it. All in all, it is a poor study with no relevance to child endangerment.

Myth: 13 children are killed each day by guns

Fact: Adults included – This "statistic" includes "children" up to age 19 or 24, depending on the source.[1] Since most violent crime is committed by males ages 16-24, the "13 children" number includes adult gang members dying during criminal activity. The proper definition of 'child' is a person between birth and puberty (typically 13-14 years old) and in 2013 only 1 child was killed on an average day nationwide, or about 0.02 children per state per day.

Fact: 411 children (age 14 and under) died from gunfire in all of 2012 or slightly more than one per day. This includes homicides, accidents, and suicides combined.[2]

Fact: Criminals are included - According to the CDC, over half of all homicides of victims aged 15-19 are gang-related. The same study found that gang-related homicides are more likely to involve firearms than those that are not (95% versus 69%).[3]

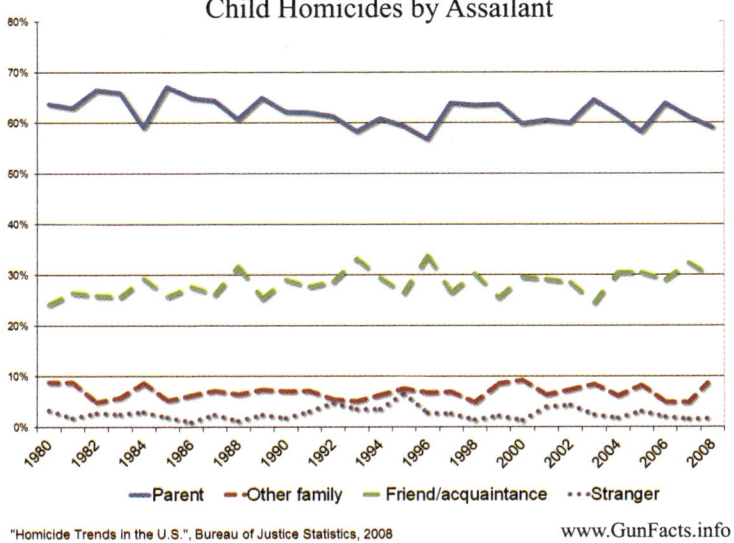

Child Homicides by Assailant

—Parent — Other family — Friend/acquaintance ···Stranger

"Homicide Trends in the U.S.", Bureau of Justice Statistics, 2008   www.GunFacts.info

Fact: Suicides are included – 26% of child firearm deaths are suicides. Hence, the "13 children" statistic includes these suicides.[4]

Fact: For contrast:

- 1,446 children die per year in transportation accidents.[5]
- Parental neglect and abuse account for 80% of all child deaths (1,274) which dwarfs gun deaths.[6]
- 1,917 children die each day from malaria[7] around the world and 15 men, women, and children per day are murdered by a convicted felon in government supervised parole/probation programs in the U.S.[8]

Myth: More Guns in U.S. Homes, More Kids Getting Shot

Fact: This study[9], published by a medical student, used a non-standard database (not official CDC records), did not analyze other variables (multi-variant analysis) and did not specify regional co-variance in gun ownership. In short, shabby science.

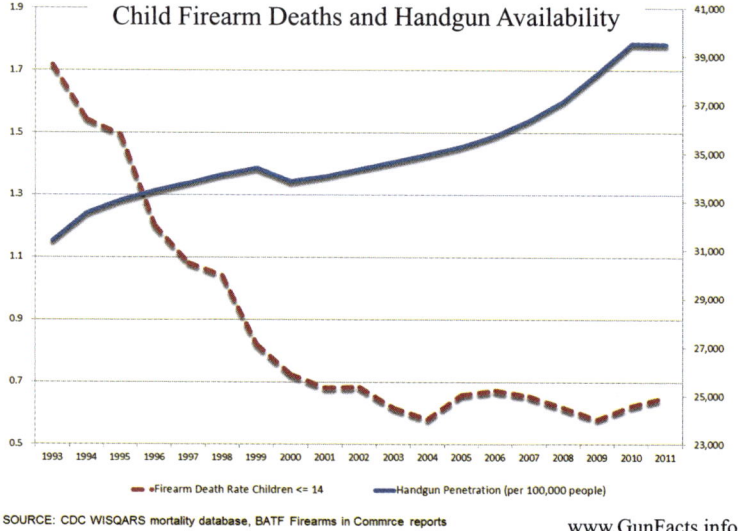

Child Firearm Deaths and Handgun Availability

●•Firearm Death Rate Children <= 14 ——Handgun Penetration (per 100,000 people)

SOURCE: CDC WISQARS mortality database, BATF Firearms in Commrce reports

www.GunFacts.info

Myth: Schoolyard shootings are an epidemic

Fact: "Compared to other types of violence and crime children face, both in and outside of school, school-based attacks are rare. While the Department of Education reports 60 million children attend the nation's 119,000 schools, available statistics indicate that few of these students will fall prey to violent situations in school settings."[10]

Fact: Over an eight-year period, in states without "right to carry" laws, there were 15 school shootings; however, in states that allow citizens to carry guns, there was only one.[11]

Fact: The five school shootings that occurred during the '97-98 school year took place after the 1995 Gun-Free School

Zones law was enacted, which banned guns within 1,000 feet of a school.[12]

Fact: Schoolyard shooting deaths are not rising, rather; they have been falling through most of the 1990s:[13]

Fact: Only 10% of public schools reported one or more serious violent crimes during the 1996-97 school year.[14]

Fact: In Pearl, Mississippi, the assistant principal carried a firearm to the school until the 1995 "Gun-Free School Zones" law passed. Afterwards he began locking his firearm in his car and parking at least a quarter-mile away from the school. In 1997, when a student began a shooting rampage, the assistant principal ran to his car, got his gun, ran back, disarmed the shooter, and held him on the ground until the police arrived. Had the law not been passed, the assistant principal might have prevented the two deaths and seven shooting-related injuries.

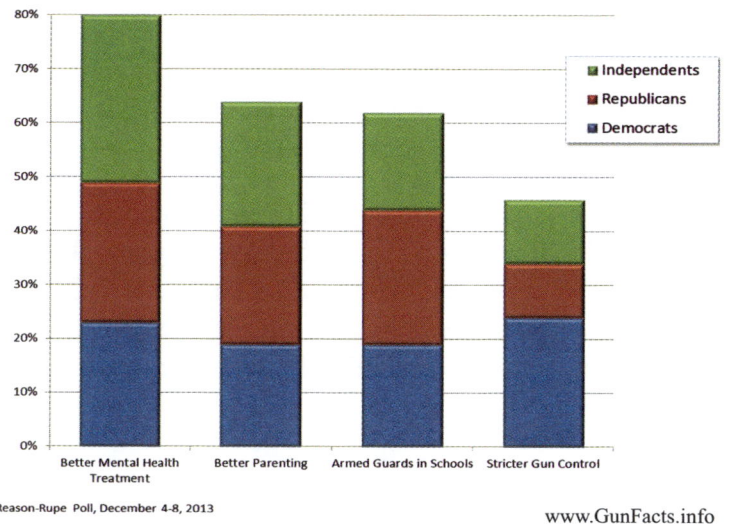

Of the following factors, which might have helped prevent the Sandy Hook Elementary School Shooting

Reason-Rupe Poll, December 4-8, 2013

www.GunFacts.info

Fact: Similar prevention occurred at a school dance in Edinboro, Pennsylvania, the Appalachian School of Law and during classes in Santee, California.

Myth: Trigger locks will keep children from accidentally shooting themselves

Fact: 31 of 32 models of gun locks tested by the government's Consumer Product Safety Commission could be opened without the key. According to their spokesperson, "We found you could open locks with paper clips, a pair of scissors or tweezers, or you could whack them on the table and they would open."[15]

Fact: 85% of all communities in America recorded no juvenile homicides in 1995, and 93.4% of communities recorded one or no juvenile arrests (not convictions) for murder.[16]

Fact: In 1996, before laws requiring trigger locks and when there were around 80 million people who owned a firearm, there were only 44 accidental gun deaths for children under age 10, or about 0.0001%.[17]

Fact: California has a trigger lock law and saw a 12% increase in fatal firearm accidents in 1994. Texas didn't have one and experienced a 28% decrease in the same year.[18]

Fact: Children as young as seven (7) years old have demonstrated that they can pick or break a trigger lock; or that they can operate a gun with a trigger lock in place.[19] Over half of non-criminal firearm deaths for children over age seven are suicides, so trigger locks are unlikely to reduce these deaths.

Fact: If criminals are deterred from attacking victims because of the fear that people might be able to defend themselves, gun locks may in turn *reduce the danger to criminals* committing crime, and thus increase crime. This problem is exacerbated because many mechanical locks (such as barrel or trigger locks) also require that the gun be stored unloaded.

Myth: Guns in America spark youth violence

Fact: Non-firearm juvenile violent crime rate in the U.S. is twice that of 25 other industrialized western nations. The non-firearm infant-homicide rate in the U.S. is 3.5 times higher.[20] Thus we have a violence problem – not a "gun" problem.

Fact: Non-firearm related homicides of children out-rank firearm related homicides by children almost 5-to-1[21]

Myth: More than 1,300 children commit suicide with guns

Fact: This statistic includes "children" ages 18-19.[22] As established previously, a child is defined as a person between birth and the age of 13 or 14 (puberty).

Fact: Worldwide, the per capita suicide rate is fairly static (the suicide rate of the U.S. is lower than many industrial countries, including many where private gun ownership is banned). A certain fraction of the population will commit suicide regardless of the available tools.

Fact: The overall rate of suicide (firearm and non-firearm) among children age 15 and under was virtually unchanged in states that passed and maintained "safe storage" laws for four or more years.[23]

Fact: Among young girls, 71% of all suicides are by hanging or suffocation.[24]

Fact: People, including children, who are determined to commit suicide will find a way. There is a documented case of a man who killed himself by drilling a hole in his skull by using a power drill.[25]

Fact: Banning country music might be more effective – one study shows 51% of the music-influenced suicide differential can be traced to country music.[26]

Comaparative Suicide Rates

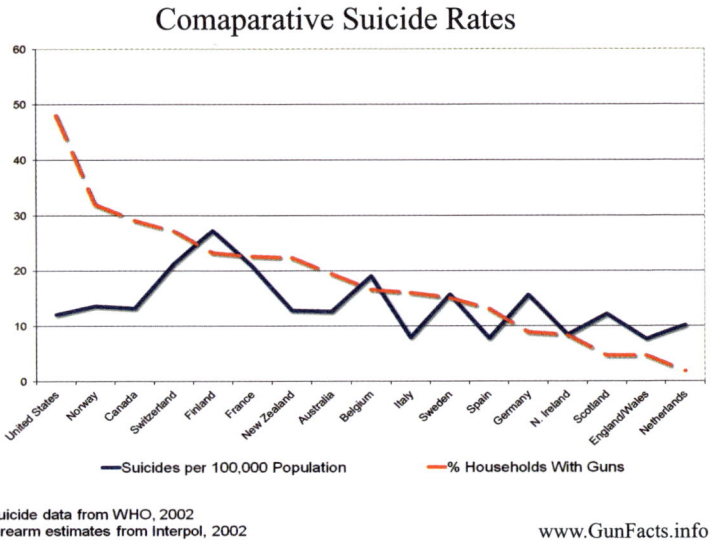

Suicide data from WHO, 2002
Firearm estimates from Interpol, 2002

www.GunFacts.info

Myth: Stricter gun control laws could have prevented the Columbine massacre

Fact: Harris and Klebold violated close to 20 firearms laws in obtaining weapons. Would 21 laws really have made a difference? The two shotguns and one rifle used by Harris and Klebold were purchased by a girlfriend who passed a background check, and the TEC-9 handgun used was already banned.

Myth: Children should be kept away from guns for their own safety

Fact: 0% of children that get guns from their parents commit gun-related crimes while 21% of those that get them illegally do.[27]

Fact: Children that acquire firearms illegally are twice as likely to commit street crimes (24%) than are those given a firearm by their parents (14%).[28]

Fact: Almost three times as many children (41%) consume illegal drugs if they also obtain firearms illegally, as compared to children given a firearm by their parents (13%).

Fact: In the 50's, children routinely played cops and robbers, had toy guns, were given BB rifles and small caliber hunting rifles before puberty. Yet the homicide rate in the 1950's was almost half of that in the 1980's.[29]

Myth: More children are shot and killed in the U.S. than anywhere else

Fact: 380 children age 14 or under were killed with firearms[30] in 2010, or 0.0005% of the children in America and barely more than one child per day. Of those, 58% of those were homicides, likely innocent bystanders in drive-by scenarios.

Myth: More children are hurt with guns than by any other means

Fact: Children are 12 times more likely to die in an automobile accident than from gun-related homicides or legal interventions (being shot by a police officer, for example) if they are age 0-14. For the group 0-24 years old (which bends the definition of "child" quite a bit), the rate is still 8.6 times higher for cars.[31]

Fact: Barely more than 1% of all unintentional deaths for children in the U.S. between ages 0-14 are from firearms.[32]

Fact: The Center for Disease Control, a federal agency, disagrees. According to them, in 1998, children 0-14 years died from the following causes in the U.S.[33]

Fact: In 2001, there were only 72 accidental firearm deaths for children under age 15, as opposed to over 2,100 children who drowned (29 times as many drowning deaths as firearm deaths).[34]

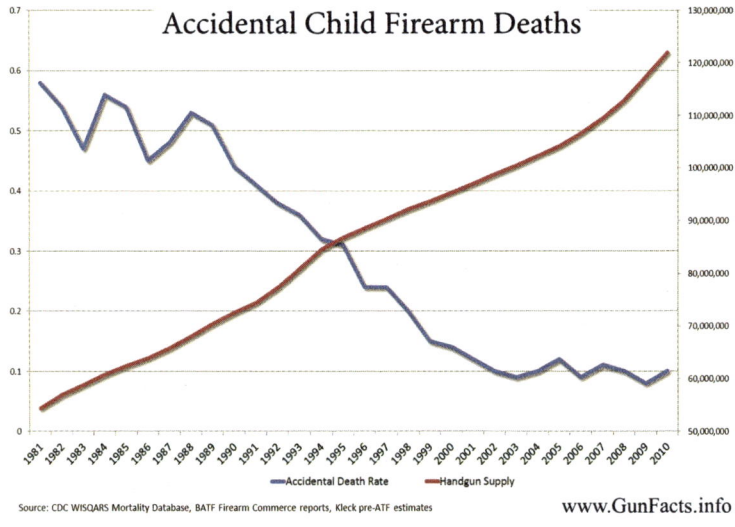

Source: CDC WISQARS Mortality Database, BATF Firearm Commerce reports, Kleck pre-ATF estimates   www.GunFacts.info

Fact: Accidental firearm injuries for children and adolescents dropped 37% from 1993 to 1997, with the fastest drop — a 64% reduction — being for children.[35]

Fact: Boys who own legal firearms have much lower rates of delinquency and drug use than non-owners of guns.[36]

Fact: The *non-gun* homicide rate of children in the U.S. is more than twice as high as in other western countries. And eight times as many children die from *non-gun* violent acts than from gun crimes.[37] This indicates that the problem is violence, not guns.

Fact: Fatal gun accidents for children ages 0-14 declined by almost 83% from 1981 to 2002[38] – all while the number of handguns per capita increased over 41%.[39]

Fact: 82% of homicides of children age 13 and under were committed *without* a gun.[40]

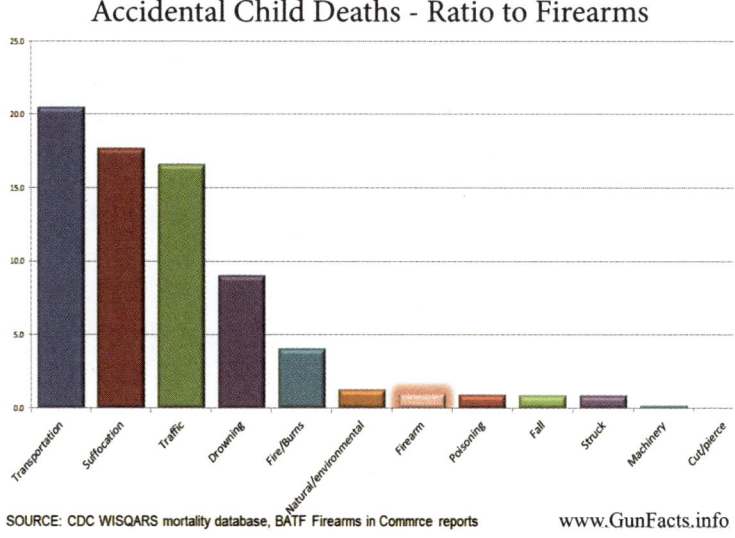

Accidental Child Deaths - Ratio to Firearms

SOURCE: CDC WISQARS mortality database, BATF Firearms in Commrce reports   www.GunFacts.info

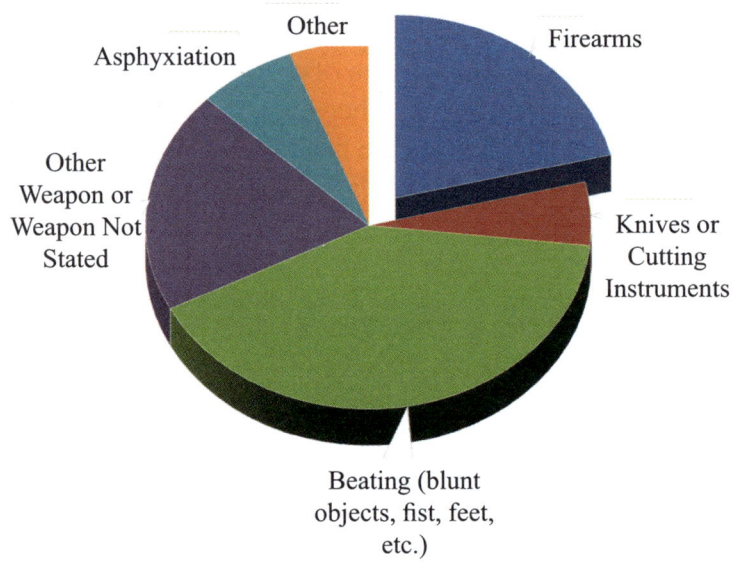

Other

Asphyxiation

Firearms

Other Weapon or Weapon Not Stated

Knives or Cutting Instruments

Beating (blunt objects, fist, feet, etc.)

SOURCE: FBI Expended Homicide Data, 2015

www.GunFacts.info

Myth: States with background checks have fewer school shootings

Fact: This was the incorrect conclusion of a very odd and extremely limited study by a medical school (not a criminology study). The study used odd and atypical control variables, but it also concluded that urban residency was a better predictor.

Myth: If it saves the life of one child, it is worth it

Fact: Firearms in private hands are used an estimated 2.5 million times (or 6,849 times each day) each year to prevent crime;[41] this includes rapes, aggravated assaults, and kidnapping. The number of innocent children protected by firearm owners far outweighs the number of children harmed.

Fact: Most Americans (firearm owners or not) believe that the way parents raise kids is what causes gun violence (or just violence in general). Among non-firearm owners, 38% said it was parental neglect that causes youth violence, while only 28% thought it was due to the availability of guns.[42] They may be right, given that most homicides of children under age five are by their own parents. Of homicides among children ages 5 and younger; 31% were killed by their own mothers and another 31% were killed by their own fathers.[43]

1. Center for Disease Control WISQARS Fatal Injury Reports for 2013
2. Center for Disease Control WISQARS Fatal Injury Reports for 2010
3. CDC Morbidity and Mortality Weekly Report: "Gang Homicides -- Five U.S. Cities, 2003-2008", published January 27, 2012
4. Center for Disease Control WISQARS Fatal Injury Reports for 2012
5. Center for Disease Control WISQARS Fatal Injury Reports for 2012
6. *Child Abuse and Neglect Fatalities 2012*, Child Welfare Information Gateway, U.S. Department of Health and Human Services
7. *Fact Sheet No 178*, U.N. World Health Organization, 1998
8. US Bureau of Justice Statistics, 1998
9. *United States Childhood Gun-Violence—Disturbing Trends*, Madenci, American Academy of Pediatrics
10. *Threat Assessment in Schools*, U.S. Secret Service and U.S. Department of Education, May 2002
11. *Multiple Victim Public Shootings, Bombings, and Right-to-Carry Concealed Handgun Laws: Contrasting Private and Public Law Enforcement*, Lott J, Landes W; University of Chicago – (covers years 1977 to 1995)
12. *Multiple Victim Public Shootings, Bombings, and Right-to-Carry Concealed Handgun Laws: Contrasting Private and Public Law Enforcement*, Lott J, Landes W; University of Chicago – (covers years 1977 to 1995)
13. *Violence and Discipline Problems in U.S. Public Schools*, National Center for Education Statistics, 1996-97
14. *Principal/School Disciplinarian Survey on School Violence*, Department of Education, March 2000

15. Washington Post, Feb 7, 2001, Page A01

16. *Crime in the United States: Uniform Crime Reports*, Federal Bureau of Investigation, 1996

17. CBS News web site, Prof. John Lott, March 20, 2000

18. National Center for Health Statistics, 1995

19. *Accidental Shootings: many deaths and injuries caused by firearms could be prevented*, United States General Accounting Office, March 1991

20. *Kids and Guns* Bulletin, Centers for Disease Control and Prevention statistics, 2000. (covers years 1990-1995)

21. FBI Uniform Crime Statistics, 1997

22. Determined using CDC mortality data, and finding the only possible fit for the claim

23. *Accidental Deaths, Suicides, and Crime Safe Storage Gun Laws*, John Lott, Yale Law School, 2000

24. *Suicide Trends Among Youths and Young Adults Aged 10--24 Years --- United States, 1990--2004*, Center for Disease Control, September 2007

25. *Drilled Head Husband Dies in Hospital*, The Scotsman, April 28, 2003

26. *The Effect of Country Music on Suicide*, Steven Stack, Jim Gundlach, Social Forces. Volume: 71. Issue: 1., 1992

27. *Urban Delinquency and Substance Abuse*, U.S. Justice Department, 2000

28. *Urban Delinquency and Substance Abuse*, U.S. Justice Department, 2000

29. *Vital Statistics*, National Center for Health Statistics, Revised July 1999

30. Center for Disease Control, WISQARS Fatal Injury Reports, 2010

31. *National Vital Statistics Report*, National Center for Health Statistics, 1997

32. *Deaths: Final Data for 2006*, National Vital Statistics Reports, 2009, Center for Disease Control

33. *Deaths: Final for 1998*, Center for Disease Control, vol. 48 no. 11., July 24, 2000

34. *20 Leading Causes of Unintentional Injury Deaths*, Center for Disease Control, United States, 2001, (All Races, Both Sexes, Ages: 1-14)

35. *Firearms Injury Surveillance Study*, Centers for Disease Control and Prevention, December 2001

36. *Urban Delinquency and Substance Abuse*, U.S. Department of Justice, National Institute of Justice, Office of Juvenile Justice and Delinquency Prevention, NCJ-143454, August 1995

37. *Kids and Guns*, Office of Juvenile Justice and Delinquency Prevention, 2000

38. National Center for Health Statistics

39. BATF estimates on handguns in circulation, BATF, Firearms Commerce in the United States 2001/2002

40. FBI Uniform Crime Statistics, 1997
41. Gary Kleck, Criminologist, Florida State University, 1997
42. Gallup/Women.com poll, May 2000
43. *FBI, Supplementary Homicide Reports*, 1976-98

Mass Shootings and Active Shooter Events

There are two criminology definitions for public shootings, and they are very different:

Active Shooter Events (ASE): Where a person shoots at multiple people in public, though there may be no deaths.[1]

Mass Public Shootings (MPS): Public shooting events where four or more people are killed.[2]

Myth: Mass public shootings are increasing

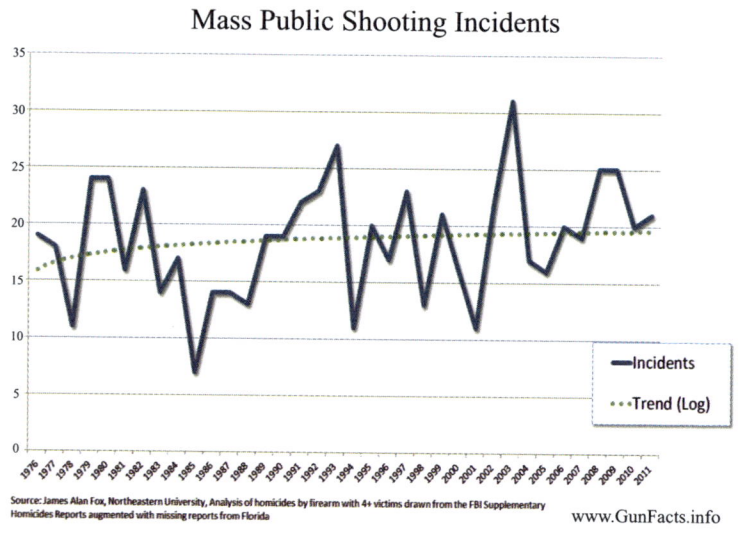

Mass Public Shooting Incidents

Source: James Alan Fox, Northeastern University, Analysis of homicides by firearm with 4+ victims drawn from the FBI Supplementary Homicides Reports augmented with missing reports from Florida

www.GunFacts.info

Fact: Over a 35-year period, the number of mass public shootings rose during the violence escalation decades of the 1970s and 1980, then leveled off, despite a growing population and greater availability for firearms (more people, more guns).

Special Note: The FBI created a study of what they labeled "active shooter" events from 2000-2013, but they merged both ASEs and MPSs. Combined, this data shows an increase whereas other studies that separate the two do not. But it must be noted that their study starts in the year 2000, which had an abnormally low number of public shootings (only one).[3]

Myth: More people are dying in mass public shootings

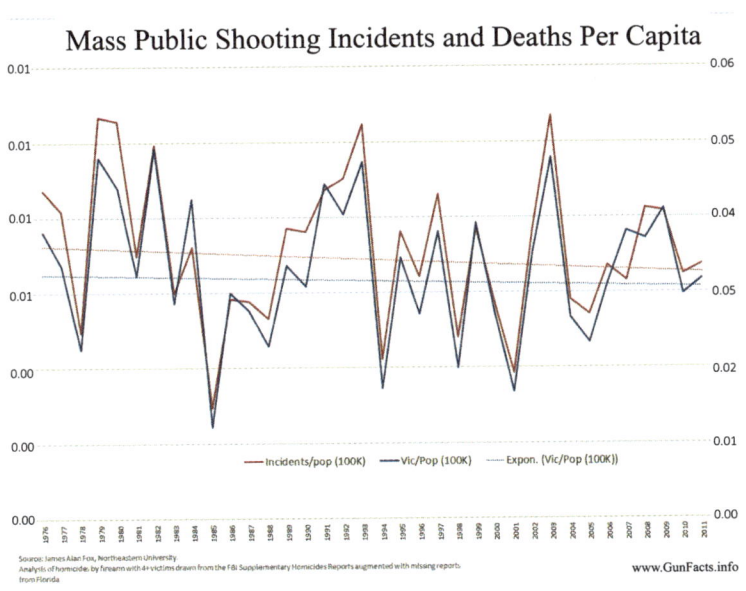

Fact: Though the raw number of mass public shootings has risen slightly over three decades, the number of people killed has *fallen* as a function of the population.

Fact: Mass public shooting deaths make up less than 1% of all gun homicides, making them a small part of the problem.

Myth: America has the highest rate of mass shootings in developed countries

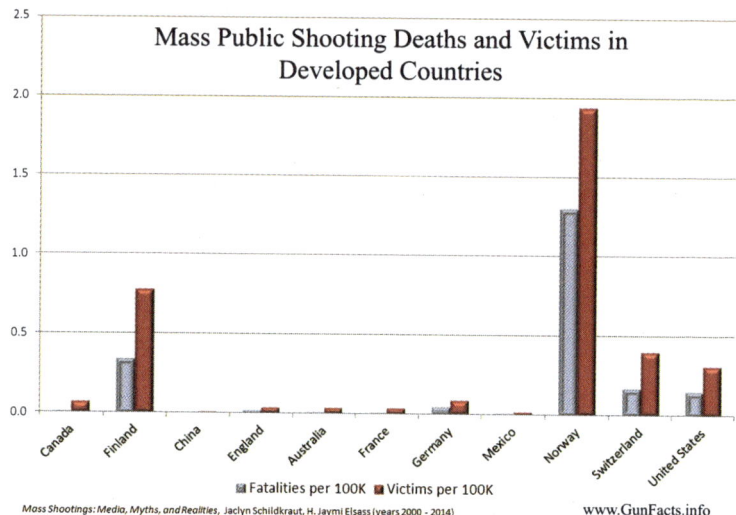

Mass Public Shooting Deaths and Victims in Developed Countries

■ Fatalities per 100K   ■ Victims per 100K

Mass Shootings: Media, Myths, and Realities, Jaclyn Schildkraut, H. Jaymi Elsass (years 2000 - 2014)   www.GunFacts.info

Fact: On a per population basis, the United States ranks fourth behind three European countries[4] or eighth when a broader set of non-conflict countries are examined.[5]

Myth: Easy access to guns creates an incentive for mass public shootings

Fact: At least 61% of mass public shooters showed signs of mental instability in the days, weeks or months before their massacres.[6] The rate might be higher because privacy laws prevent fully exploring the mental health history of some killers. Mental health is the determinant variable.

Myth: Guns in civilian hands are not good for stopping mass public shooters

Fact: One study shows that armed citizens responding to rampage killers result in 1/8th the number of casualties than when police intervene.[7] In other words, waiting on the police results in eight times as many people deaths and injuries.

Understanding conflicting reports on "mass public shootings"

There are several different studies concerning mass public shootings, which make different claims. The primary points of confusion come from:

1. How the counting of such shootings is done
2. How they define "mass public shooting"

Here are some of the studies that are circulated and critiques of them.

Mother Jones[8]

- This magazine article used only media reports of mass shootings, which may not cover all such shootings and which lack criminological objectivity.

- There appear to be some arbitrary omissions of events that do not fit their definition of a public shooting.

- They only count "lone gunmen" events, and never the more common inner-city, gang-related multi-shooter episodes.

- They include terrorist activities, such as the Fort Hood massacre.

Mother Jones concluded that mass shootings occur more frequently than several decades ago, and that the mass public shooting rate tripled since 2011.

James Alan Fox, Northeastern University criminologist[9]

- Based on police reports, which are uniform and comprehensive.

- Includes all mass shootings, including those not in public, which defies the idea of a mass public shooting.

Concluded that mass shooting has remained relatively stable over time.

Grant Duwe, Minnesota Department of Corrections, criminologist[10]

- Uses FBI Supplementary Homicide Reports for the core list, then media reports to provide details.

- Includes only public events.

- Excludes events related to other crimes (such as robberies gone wrong).

Concludes that mass public shootings declined from 1999 to 2011, then spiked in 2012 (the year of the Sandy Hook Elementary School shooting), then returned to the mean of previous years.

The one thing all of the studies agree upon is that mass public shootings are statistically rare

1. "One or more persons engaged in killing or attempting to kill multiple people in an area (or areas) occupied by multiple unrelated individuals. At least one of the victims must be unrelated to the shooter. The primary motive appears to be mass murder; that is the shooting is not a by-product of an attempt to commit another crime." *United States Active Shooter Events from 2000 to 2010*, School of Criminal Justice, Texas State University, 2014 – published by the Federal Bureau of Investigation
2. "Slaughter of four or more victims by one or a few assailants within a single event, lasting but a few minutes or as long as several

hours", *Multiple Homicide: Patterns of Serial and Mass Murder*, James Alan Fox, Jack Levin, Crime and Justice, Vol. 23, 1998

3. *A Study of Active Shooter Incidents in the United States Between 2000 and 2013*, FBI, September 2013

4. *Mass Shootings: Media, Myths, and Realities*, Jaclyn Schildkraut, H. Jaymi Elsass

5. *The facts shoot holes in Obama's claim that US is only host to mass killings*, John Lott, December 2015

6. *Mass Shootings: Maybe What We Need Is a Better Mental-Health Policy*, Mother Jones, Nov 2012, analysis of 62 mass public shootings

7. *Auditing Shooting Rampage Statistics*, Davi Barker, July 2013 and updated thereafter

8. *A Guide to Mass Shootings in America*, Mother Jones, May 2014

9. *Mass Shootings in America: Moving Beyond Newtown*, Homicide Studies, 2013

10. *Mass Murder in the United States: A History*, McFarland, June 2007

Accidental Death and Injuries

Myth: Accidental gun fatalities are a serious problem

Fact: Firearm misuse causes only a small number of accidental deaths in the U.S.[1] For example, compared to being accidentally killed by a firearm, you are:

Five times more likely to burn to death

Five times more likely to drown

- 17 times more likely to be poisoned
- 17 times more likely to fall to your death
- And 68 times more likely to die in an automobile accident

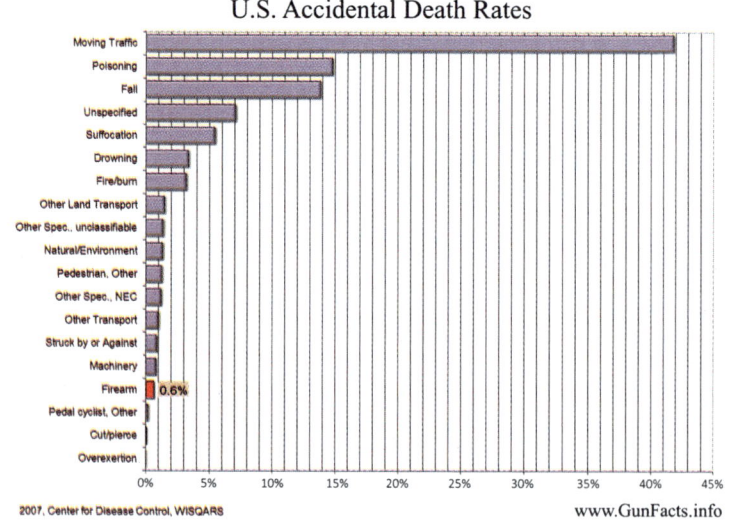

U.S. Accidental Death Rates

2007, Center for Disease Control, WISQARS

www.GunFacts.info

Fact: In 2007, there were only 54 accidental gun deaths for children under age 13. About 12 times as many children died from drowning during the same period.[2]

Fact: In 2007, there were 999 drowning victims and 137 firearm-related accidental deaths in age groups 1 through 19. This despite the fact that firearms outnumber pools by a factor of more than 30:1. Thus, the risk ratio of drowning in an available pool is nearly 100 times higher than dying from a firearm-related accident for all ages, and nearly 500 times for children ages 0-5.[3]

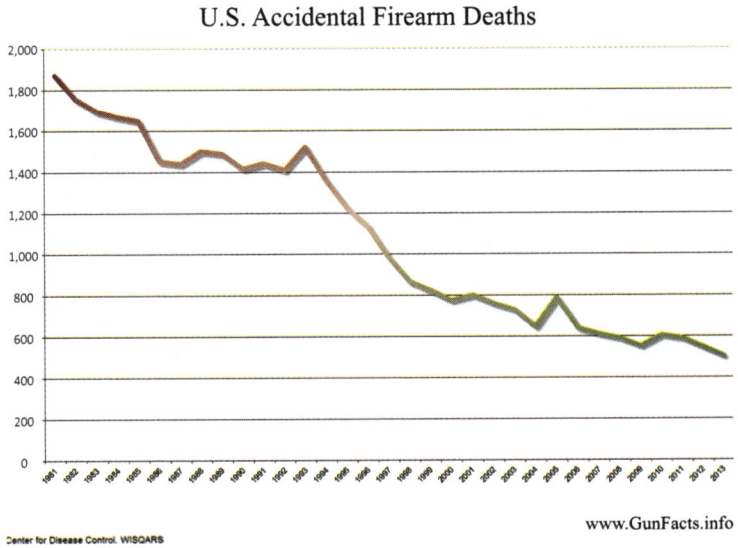

U.S. Accidental Firearm Deaths

Center for Disease Control. WISQARS

www.GunFacts.info

Fact: Medical mistakes kill 400,000 people per year – the equivalent of almost three fully loaded Boeing 747 jet crashes per day – or about 286 times the rate of all accidental firearm deaths.[4] This translates into 1 in 6 doctors causing an accidental death, and 1 in 56,666 gun owners doing the same.

Fact: Only 2% of gun deaths are from accidents, and some insurance investigations indicate that many of these may not be accidents after all.[5]

Fact: Around 2,000 patients each year — six per day — are accidentally killed or injured in hospitals by registered nurses.[6]

Myth: Handguns are unsafe and cause accidents

Fact: Most fatal firearm accidents involve long guns, which are more deadly. These are typically hunting accidents.[7]

Fact: Handguns have triggers that are difficult for small (child) hands to operate, and are rarely the cause of accidents.[8]

Myth: Innocent bystanders are often killed by guns

Fact: Less than 1% of all gun homicides involve innocent bystanders.[9]

Myth: Citizens are too incompetent to use guns for protection

Fact: About 11% of police shootings kill an innocent person — about 2% of shootings by citizens kill an innocent person. The odds of a defensive gun user killing an innocent person are less than 1 in 26,000[10] despite American citizens using guns to prevent crimes almost 2,500,000 times every year.

Fact: Most firearm accidents are caused by people with various forms of poor self-control. These include alcoholics, people with previous criminal records, people with multiple driving accidents, and people who engage in other risky behaviors.[11]

Myth: Gun accidents are flooding emergency rooms

Fact: The rate of gun accidents is so low that the U.S. Consumer Product Safety Commission doesn't even mention them in their annual safety reports.

Myth: "Junk" guns are dangerous and should be banned

Fact: In the history of the state of California, not one lawsuit against a gun maker had been filed (until 2003) based on a weapon being defective or poorly designed.[12]

Myth: Guns should be made to conform to product liability laws

Fact: Guns are already covered under product liability laws. If you have a defective gun that does not operate properly, you can sue the gun maker.

1. *WISQARS Injury Mortality Report*, Center for Disease Control, 2007
2. *WISQARS Injury Mortality Report*, Center for Disease Control, 2007
3. National Center for Health Statistics, and the National Spa and Pool Institute
4. *Medical death statistics, Gun deaths*, Dr. David Lawrence, CEO Kaiser Permanente, CDC report 1993
5. *Targeting Guns: Firearms and Their Control*, Gary Kleck, Aldine de Gruyter 1997 at 293-324
6. Chicago Tribune report, Sept 10, 2000
7. *Targeting Guns: Firearms and Their Control*, Gary Kleck, Aldine de Gruyter 1997, at 293-324
8. *Targeting Guns: Firearms and Their Control*, Gary Kleck, Aldine de Gruyter 1997, at 293-324
9. *Stray bullets and 'mushrooms'*, Sherman, Steele, Laufersweiler, Hoffer and Julian, Journal of Quantitative Criminology, 1989
10. *Shall Issue: The New Wave of Concealed Handgun Permit Laws,* C. Cramer, and D. Kopel, Independence Institute Issue Paper. October 17,

1994

11. *Targeting Guns: Firearms and Their Control*, Gary Kleck, Aldine de Gruyter, 1997, at 307, 312

12. California Trial Lawyers Association, 1998

Availability of Guns

Myth: The availability of guns causes crime

Fact: Though the number of firearms owned by private citizens has been increasing steadily since 1970, the overall rate of homicides and suicides has not risen (though suicide rates did start to rise during the Great Recession).[1] As the chart shows, there is no correlation between the availability of firearms and the rates of homicide and suicide in America.

Fact: Internationally speaking "There's no clear relationship between more guns and higher levels of violence."[2]

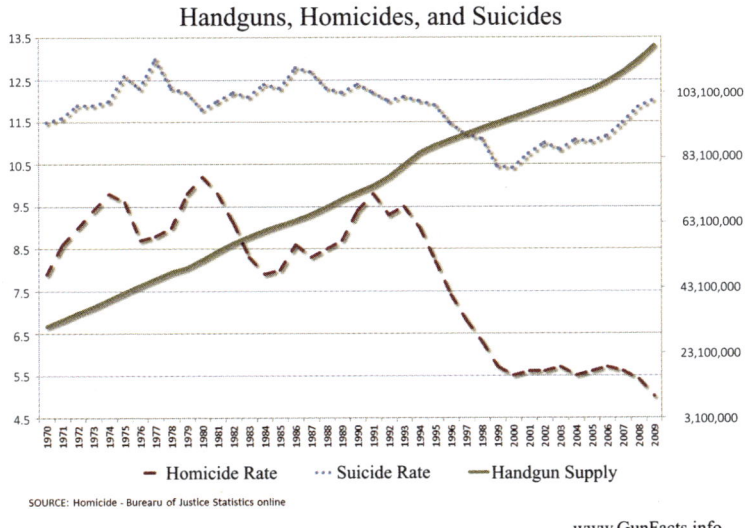

Handguns, Homicides, and Suicides

— Homicide Rate   ⋯ Suicide Rate   — Handgun Supply

SOURCE: Homicide - Bureau of Justice Statistics online

www.GunFacts.info

Fact: "A detailed study of the major surveys completed in the past 20 years or more provides no evidence of any relationship between the total number of legally held firearms in society and the rate of armed crime. Nor is there a relationship between the severity of controls imposed in various countries or the mass of bureaucracy involved with many control systems with the apparent ease of access to firearms by criminals and terrorists."[3]

Fact: Handgun ownership among groups normally associated with higher violent crime (young males, blacks, low income, inner city, etc.) is at or below national averages.[4]

Fact: Among inmates who used a firearm in the commission of a crime, the most significant correlations occurred when the inmates' parents abused drugs (27.5%) and when inmates had friends engaged in illegal activities (32.5% for robberies, 24.3% for drug trafficking). [5]

Fact: Five out of six gun-possessing felons obtained handguns from the secondary market and by theft, and "[the] criminal handgun market is overwhelmingly dominated by informal transactions and theft as mechanisms of supply."[6]

Fact: The majority of handguns in the possession of criminals are stolen, and not necessarily by the criminals in question.[7] In fact, over 100,000 firearms are stolen in burglaries every year, and most of them likely enter the criminal market (i.e., are sold or traded to criminals).[8]

Fact: In 1968, the U.K. passed laws that reduced the number of licensed firearm owners, and thus reduced firearm availability. U.K. homicide rates **have steadily risen** since then.[9] Ironically, firearm use in crimes has ***doubled*** in the decade after the U.K. banned handguns.[10]

Fact: Most violent crime is caused by a small minority of repeat offenders. One California study found that 3.8% of a group of males born in 1956 were responsible for 55.5% of all serious felonies.[11] 75-80% of murder arrestees have prior arrests for a violent (including non-fatal) felony or burglary. On average, they have about four felony arrests and one felony conviction.

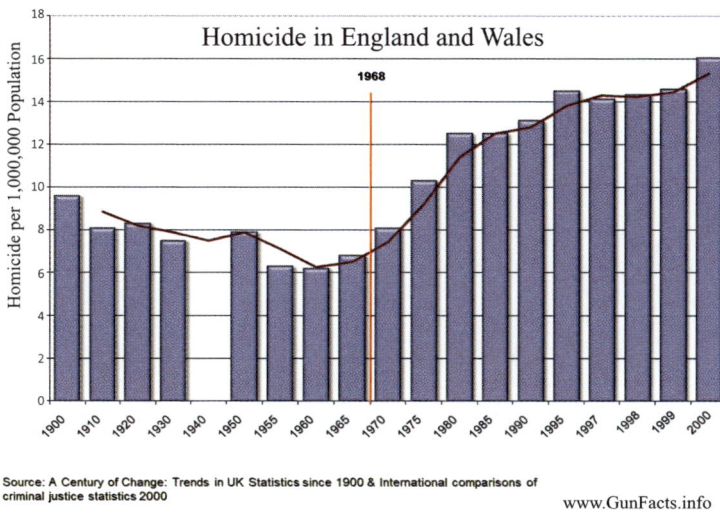

Homicide in England and Wales

Source: A Century of Change: Trends in UK Statistics since 1900 & International comparisons of criminal justice statistics 2000

www.GunFacts.info

Fact: Half of all murders are committed by people on "conditional release" (i.e., parole or probation).[12] 81% of all homicide defendants had an arrest record, 67% had a felony arrest record, 70% had a conviction record, and 54% had a felony conviction.[13]

Fact: Per capita firearm ownership rates have risen steadily since 1959 while crime rates have gone up and down depending on economics, drug trafficking innovations, and "get tough" crime legislation.[14]

Thoughts: Criminals are not motivated by guns. They are motivated by opportunity. Attempts to reduce public access to firearms provide criminals more points of opportunity. It is little wonder that high-crime cities also tend to be those with the most restrictive gun control laws – which criminals tend to ignore.

Myth: Gun availability increases suicide rates

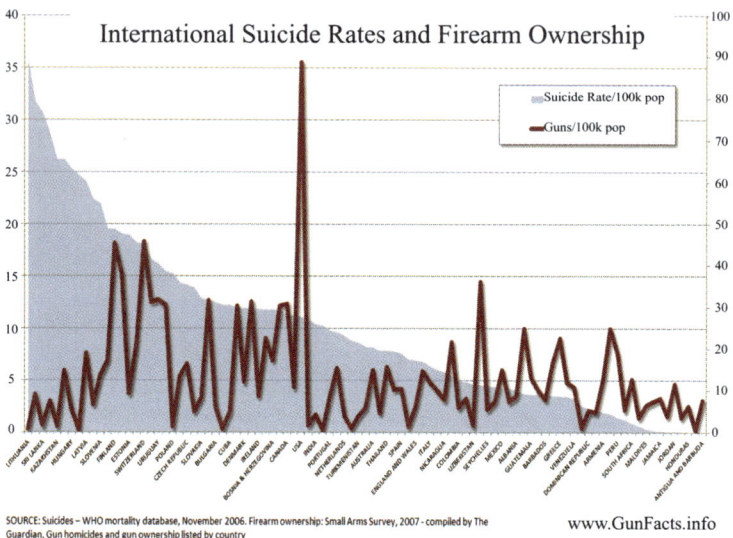

International Suicide Rates and Firearm Ownership

Suicide Rate/100k pop
Guns/100k pop

SOURCE: Suicides – WHO mortality database, November 2006. Firearm ownership: Small Arms Survey, 2007 - compiled by The Guardian, Gun homicides and gun ownership listed by country

www.GunFacts.info

Fact: Cross national studies show that there is no relationship to suicides rates and the availability of firearms. Two outstanding contrasts:

- The U.S. and Canada – who share geography, cultural elements, and entertainment – have nearly identical suicide rates, but Canada has significantly lower gun ownership.
- Lithuania – which has nearly zero-gun ownership – has the world's highest suicide rate, more than three times that of the United States.

Myth: Gun availability is what is causing school shootings

Fact: Schoolyard shootings have been occurring since at least 1974, so it is not a new phenomenon due to increases in gun ownership.[15]

SAF Debate Book

Fact: More than 50% of these murderers started thinking about their assaults two or more weeks before the shooting, and 75% planned-out their attacks, showing that these events are not spontaneous.[16]

Thoughts: In rural areas, guns are everywhere, and children are taught to shoot at young ages – yet these areas are almost devoid of schoolyard shootings. Clearly, availability is not the issue.

Myth: Gun availability leads to massacres

Fact: In 62% of mass public shootings, the assailant had a history of having "displayed signs of mental health problems prior to the killings."[17]

Myth: Gun ownership is linked to higher homicide rates

Fact: This "study"[18] has multiple defects which, when corrected, reverse the results. Some of the defects of this study include:

- Exclusion of the District of Columbia, a high crime city
- Use of other crime rates to indirectly explain homicide rates
- Use of purely cross-sectional data that never allowed control variable analysis
- Data from different years is used without any explanation (unemployment rate from 2000 to explain the homicide rate from 2001 to 2003, etc.).

Myth: Handguns are 43 times more likely to kill a family member than a criminal

Fact: Of the 43 deaths reported in this flawed study, 37 (86%) were suicides. Other deaths involved criminal activity between the family members (botched drug deals).[19]

Fact: Of the remaining deaths, the deceased family members include felons, drug dealers, violent spouses committing assault, and other criminals.[20]

Fact: Only 0.1% of the defensive uses of guns results in the death of the predator.[21] This means you are much more likely to prevent a crime without bloodshed than hurt a family member.

1. *Targeting Guns: Firearms and Their Control*, Gary Kleck, Aldine de Gruyter, 1997. (With supporting data from the FBI Uniform Crime Statistics, 1972 to 1995.)
2. *Small Arms Survey Project*, Keith Krause, Graduate Institute of International Studies, Geneva, 2007
3. *Minutes of Evidence*, Colin Greenwood, Select Committee on Northern Ireland Affairs, January 29, 2003
4. *Targeting Guns: Firearms and Their Control*, Gary Kleck, Aldine de Gruyter, 1997. (Ownership tables derived from the annual "General Social Survey.")
5. *Firearm Use by Offenders*, Bureau of Justice Statistics, November 2001
6. *The Armed Criminal in America: A Survey of Incarcerated Felons*, James D. Wright, Peter H. Rossi, National Institute of Justice (U.S.), 1985
7. *Targeting Guns: Firearms and Their Control,* Gary Kleck, Aldine de Gruyter, 1997.
8. *Victimization During Household Burglary*, Bureau of Justice Statistics, September 2010
9. *A Century of Change: Trends in UK Statistics since 1900*, Hicks, Joe; Allen, Grahame (SGS), Social and General Statistics Section, House of Commons
10. *Weapons sell for just £50 as suspects and victims grow ever younger*, The Times, August 24, 2007
11. *The Prevalence and Incidence of Arrest Among Adult Males in California*, Robert Tillman, prepared for California Department of Justice, Bureau of Criminal Statistics and Special Services, Sacramento, California, 1987
12. *Probation and Parole Violators in State Prison, 1991: Survey of State Prison Inmates*, Robyn Cohen, U.S. Dept. of Justice, Office of Justice Programs, Bureau of Justice Statistics, 1995
13. *Felony Defendants in Large Urban Counties*, 1998, Brian Reaves, U.S. Department of Justice, Office of Justice Programs, Bureau of Justice Statistics, November 2001

14. *Felony Defendants in Large Urban Counties*, 1998, Brian Reaves, U.S. Department of Justice, Office of Justice Programs, Bureau of Justice Statistics, November 2001 (Based on a compilation of 85 separate surveys from 1959 through 1996.)

15. *U.S.S.S. Safe School Initiative: An Interim Report on the Prevention of Targeted Violence in Schools*, B. Vossekuil, M. Reddy, R. Fein, R. Borum, W. Modzeleski, U. S. Secret Service, Threat Assessment Center, 2000

16. *U.S.S.S. Safe School Initiative: An Interim Report on the Prevention of Targeted Violence in Schools*, B. Vossekuil, M. Reddy, R. Fein, R. Borum, W. Modzeleski, U. S. Secret Service, Threat Assessment Center, 2000

17. *Mass Shootings: Maybe What We Need Is a Better Mental-Health Policy*, Mother Jones, November 9, 2012

18. *State-level homicide victimization rates in the US in relation to survey measures of household firearm ownership, 2001–2003*, Matthew Miller, David Hemenway, Deborah Azrael, Harvard School of Public Health, October 27, 2006

19. *Protection or Peril? An Analysis of Firearm-Related Deaths in the Home*, Arthur L. Kellerman, D.T. Reay, 314 New Eng. J. Med. 1557-60, June 12, 1986. (Kellerman admits that his study did "not include cases in which burglars or intruders are wounded or frightened away by the use or display of a firearm." He also admitted his study did not look at situations in which intruders "purposely avoided a home known to be armed." This is a classic case of a "study" conducted to achieve a desired result. In his critique of this "study", Gary Kleck notes that the estimation of gun ownership rates was "inaccurate", and that the total population came from a non-random selection of only two cities.)

20. *Protection or Peril? An Analysis of Firearm-Related Deaths in the Home*, Arthur L. Kellerman, D.T. Reay, 314 New Eng. J. Med. 1557-60, June 12, 1986

21. *Point Blank: Guns and Violence in America*, Gary Kleck, New York: Aldine de Gruyter, 1991

Government, Laws, Social Costs

Myth: Gun control reduces crime

Fact: There are more than 22,000[1] gun laws at the city, county, state, and federal level. If gun control worked, then we should be free of crime. Yet the U.S. government "found insufficient evidence to determine the effectiveness of any of the firearms laws or combinations of laws reviewed on violent outcomes"[2] and also concluded in one study that none of the attackers interviewed was "hindered by any law – federal, state or local –that has ever been established to prevent gun ownership. They just laughed at gun laws."[3]

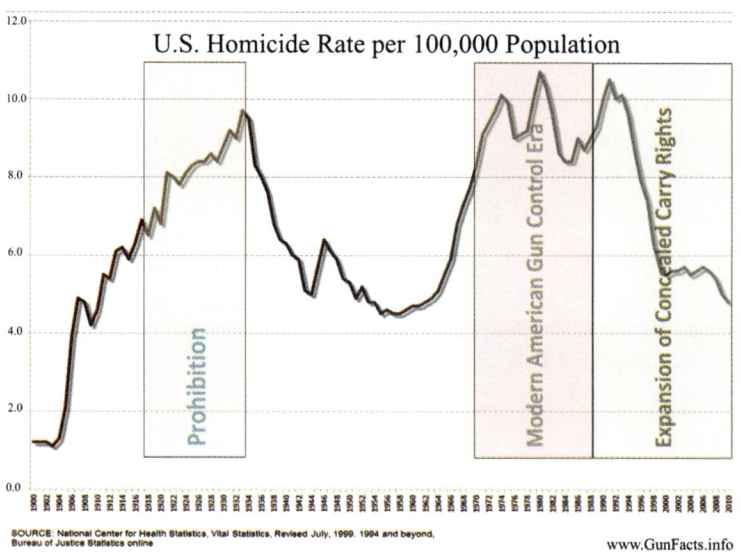

U.S. Homicide Rate per 100,000 Population

SOURCE: National Center for Health Statistics, Vital Statistics, Revised July, 1999, 1994 and beyond.
Bureau of Justice Statistics online

www.GunFacts.info

Fact: Violent crime appears to be encouraged by gun control. Most gun control laws in the United States have been written since 1968, yet the murder rate rose during the 70s, 80s and early 90s.[4]

Fact: In 1976, Washington, D.C. enacted one of the most restrictive gun control laws in the nation. The city's murder rate rose 134 percent through 1996 while the national murder rate dropped 2 percent.[5]

Fact: Among the 15 states with the highest homicide rates, 10 have restrictive or very restrictive gun laws.[6]

Fact: Maryland claims to have the toughest gun control laws in the nation and ranks #1 in robberies and #4 in both violent crime and murder.[7] The robbery rate is 70% more than the national average.[8] These numbers are likely low because one of their more violent cities, Baltimore, failed to report their crime levels.

Fact: In 2000, 20% of U.S. homicides occurred in four cities with just six percent of the population – New York, Chicago, Detroit, and Washington, D.C. – most of which had a virtual prohibition on privately owned handguns at the time.[9]

Fact: The landmark federal Gun Control Act of 1968, banning most interstate gun sales, had no discernible impact on the criminal acquisition of guns from other states.[10]

Fact: Washington, D.C.'s 1976 ban on the ownership of handguns (except those already registered in the District) was not linked to any reduction in gun crime in the nation's capital.[11]

Fact: New York has one of the most restrictive gun laws in the nation – and 20% of the armed robberies.[12]

Fact: In analyzing 10 different possible reasons for the decline in violent crime during the 1990s, gun control was calculated to have contributed nothing (high imprisonment rates, more police and legalized abortion were considered the primary factors, contributing as much as 28% of the overall reduction).[13]

Gun Facts & Myth 77

Myth: The Brady Bill caused a decrease in gun homicides

Fact: All violent crime (including gun and non-gun murders) fell during the same period, 1992 to 1997. However, the percent of homicides committed with guns stayed the same. In 1992, 68% of murders were committed with guns; in 1997, it was still 68%.[14] Thus, the decreased gun homicide rate was part of an overall declining crime rate, not an effect of the Brady Bill.

Fact: Gun possession by criminals has risen in the post-Brady years – 18% of state prisoners (was 16% before Brady) and 15% of federal prisoners (was 12% before Brady) were caught with firearms.[15]

Fact: The Brady Bill is not enforced. In 2006, of 77,000 Field Office referrals for instant background check violations (25,259 of which NICS identified as buyers with felony records), 0.4% (273) were ever charged with a crime and 0.1% (73) were convicted.[16]

Fact: The Brady Bill has so far failed to appreciably save lives.[17]

Fact: Violent crime started falling in 1991, three years before passage of the Brady Bill. The Brady Bill did not apply in 18 states, yet violent crime in those states fell just as quickly.[18]

Fact: A majority of Americans agree that the bill is worthless. 51% believe the act has been ineffective at reducing violent crime, and 56% believe it has had no impact on reducing the number of homicides in the U.S.[19]

Myth: California's tough gun laws reduced gun deaths

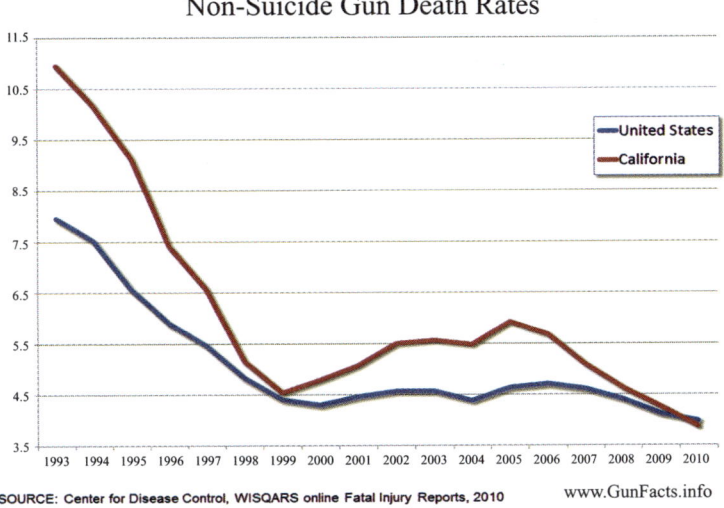

Non-Suicide Gun Death Rates

Legend: United States, California

SOURCE: Center for Disease Control, WISQARS online Fatal Injury Reports, 2010   www.GunFacts.info

This myth, promoted primarily by the Law Center to Prevent Gun Violence and covering years 1993 through 2013, has three major flaws:

- Suicides, which are 61%[20] of gun deaths, fell much faster in California than the rest of the nation.
- At the starting point, California's criminal gun death rate was much higher than the national average.
- California passed the first of two "three strikes" laws in 1994, which began the process of incarcerating repeat violent offenders.

Thus, none of the decline in California gun deaths is attributable to the state's gun control laws.

Myth: Gun laws are being enforced

Fact: During the Clinton administration, federal prosecutions of gun-related crimes dropped more than 44 percent.[21]

Fact: Of the 3,353 prohibited individuals that obtained firearms, the Clinton administration only investigated 110 of them (3.3%).[22]

Fact: Despite 536,000 prohibited buyers caught by the National Instant (Criminal Background) Check System (NICS), only 6,700 people (1.25%) have been charged for these firearms violations. This includes 71% of the violations coming from convicted or indicted felons.[23] None of these crimes were prosecuted by the Federal government in 1996, 1997, or 1998.[24]

Fact: In 1998, the government prosecuted just eight children for gun law violations.[25] In that same year, there were only:

- 8 prosecutions for juvenile handgun possession.
- 6 prosecutions for handgun transfer to juveniles.
- 1 prosecution for Brady Bill violations.

Fact: Some of the reasons listed for not prosecuting known gun criminals include "minimal federal interest" and "DOJ/ U.S. Attorney policy".[26]

Fact: Half of referrals concerning violent criminals were closed without investigation or prosecution.[27]

Fact: The average sentence for a federal firearms violation dropped from 57 months to 46 months from 1996 to 1998.[28]

Fact: 18-20 year-olds commit over 23% of all gun murders.[29] None of these criminals are allowed by law to purchase a handgun, but the Federal government under Clinton rarely enforced this law.[30]

Fact: During Project Exile in Richmond, Virginia, US and State authorities prosecuted felons caught with guns, using Federal laws that require mandatory imprisonment. The first-year result was a 33% drop in homicides for the Richmond Metro area in a year where the national murder rate was climbing.[31] This shows that enforcement works. According to Andrew McBride of the Richmond Department of Justice, these cases are as easy to prosecute as "picking change up off the street."

Myth: Federal gun crime prosecutions increased 25%

Fact: 1992: 9,885 BATF referrals for federal firearm purchase violations

1998: 4,391 (a 56% drop)

1999: 5,489 (a fictitious "25% increase")[32]

Fact: 1992: 12,084 BATF referrals for all firearm law violations

1998: 5,620 (a 53% drop)

Myth: The social cost of gun violence is enormous

Fact: Because guns are used an estimated 2.5 million times per year to *prevent* crimes, the cost savings in personal losses, police work, and court and prison expenses vastly outweighs the cost of criminal gun violence and gun accidents. The net savings, under a worst-case scenario, is about $3.5 billion a year.[33]

Fact: Guns are used 65 times more often to prevent a crime than to commit one.[34]

Fact: The medical cost of gun violence is only 0.16% of America's annual health care expenditures.[35]

Fact: Drunken drivers killed 15,935 people in 1998[36] while homicides with guns were 12,102 for the same year. Drunken drivers continue to kill people randomly despite a decade of increased strictness and social pressure against drunk drivers.

Myth: The social cost of gun violence is $20-100 billion

Fact: One "study"[37] included the lifetime earnings of people that die from guns, not just the true social costs. This included lost incomes of criminals killed by law-abiding citizens, costs associated with suicides, the "emotional costs experienced by relatives and friends of gunshot victims, and the fear and general reduction in quality of life ... including people who are not victimized". If the same methodology were used to calculate the social savings from private gun ownership, we would see a benefit to society of half a trillion dollars, or 10% of the 1999 US Gross Domestic Product.

Fact: Another "study"[38] started by polling people how much they would be willing to have their taxes raised in order to reduce firearm violence by 30%, and then projected these bids to the entire U.S. population. This seriously flawed methodology does not measure the "cost" of the problem, just what people are willing to spend to reduce the problem.

Fact: Social saving from private ownership is not used in these studies. One study[39] indicated between 240,000 and 300,000 defensive uses of firearms, as described by the victim, "... almost certainly had saved a life."

Myth: Gun "buy-back" programs get guns off the streets

Fact: According to the federal government, gun 'buy-backs' have "no effect".[40]

Fact: "Buy-backs" remove no more than 2% of the firearms within a community. And the firearms that are removed do not resemble guns used in crimes. *"There has never been any effect on crime results seen"*.[41]

Fact: Up to 62% of people trading in a firearm still have another at home, and 27% said they would or might buy another within a year.[42]

Fact: More than 50% of the weapons bought via a gun buyback program were over 15 years old, whereas almost half of firearms seized from juveniles are less than three years old.[43]

Fact: 81% of police surveyed believe buy-backs are ineffective in reducing gun violence.[44]

Fact: According to a variety of sources, the actual effect is that gun buy-back programs:

- Disarm future crime victims, creating new social costs
- Give criminals an easy way to dispose of evidence
- Acquire guns from those least likely to commit crimes (the elderly, women, etc.)
- Result in cheap guns being bought by private individuals and sold to the government for a profit
- Cause guns to be stolen and sold to the police, creating more crime
- Seldom return stolen guns to their rightful owners

Fact: "They do very little good. Guns arriving at buy-backs are simply not the same guns that would otherwise have been used in crime. If you look at the people who are turning in firearms, they are consistently the least crime-prone [ed: least likely to commit crimes]: older people and women."[45]

Myth: Closing down "kitchen table" gun dealers will reduce guns on the street

Fact: 43% of gun dealers had no inventory and sold no guns at all. Congressional testimony documented that the large number of low-volume gun dealers is a direct result of BATF policy. The BATF once prosecuted gun collectors who sold as few as three guns per year at gun shows, claiming that they were unlicensed, and therefore illegal, gun dealers. To avoid such harassment, thousands of American gun collectors became licensed gun dealers. Now the BATF claims not to have the resources to audit the paperwork monster it created.

Fact: Reforms of the Federal Firearm Licensing program – mainly focused at small volume retailers and traders – produced no significant results in firearm crime rates.[46]

Myth: Only the government should have guns

Fact: Only if you want criminals to have them as well. Loose inventory controls are notorious in government agencies, as shown by the Immigration and Naturalization Service (INS) that has "misplaced" 539 weapons, including a gas-grenade launcher and 39 automatic rifles or machine guns. Six guns were eventually linked to crimes (two guns had been used in armed robberies, one was confiscated in a raid on a drug laboratory, two others during arrests and one was being held as evidence in a homicide investigation).[47] In July of 2001, it was reported that the FBI lost 449 weapons, including machine guns.

Myth: "Safe storage" laws protect people

Fact: Fifteen states that passed "safe storage" laws saw 300 more murders, 3,860 more rapes, 24,650 more robberies, and over 25,000 more aggravated assaults in the first five years. On average, the annual costs borne by victims averaged over $2.6 billion as a result of lost productivity, out-of-pocket expenses, medical bills, and property losses. "The problem is, you see no decrease in either juvenile accidental gun deaths or suicides when such laws are enacted, but you do see an increase in crime rates."[48]

Fact: Only five American children under the age of 10 died of accidents involving handguns in 1997.[49] Thus, the need for "safe storage" laws appears to be low.

Fact: In Merced California, an intruder stabbed three children to death with a pitchfork. The oldest child had been trained by her father in firearms use, but could not save her siblings from the attacker because the gun was locked away to comply with the state's "safe storage" law.[50]

Myth: Local background checks reduce gun suicides[51]

Fact: The research reports only a change in the "firearm suicide rate" and not the total suicide rate. No strict correlation between overall suicides and background checks exists.

Fact: The report did not explain the disparity between states that had local background checks and radically different suicide rates (Hawaii with 2.82/100,000 and Washington with 9.28/100,000). Nor did it explain how states with different levels of background checks have nearly identical suicide rates (Hawaii has local checks and a 2.82 firearm suicide rate while New York uses state checks and has a lower 2.72 rate).

Fact: The report was a two-year snapshot, which makes trending impossible. Proper analysis would have examined change in suicide rates in states before and after background check policy changed.

Fact: Researchers split homicide and suicide propensity controls by age (65+ for suicides and 15-29 for homicides).

1. *Under the Gun: Weapons, Crime, and Violence in America*, Bureau of Alcohol, Tobacco and Firearms estimate and reported via James Wright, Peter H. Rossi, Kathleen Daly, 1983
2. *First Reports Evaluating the Effectiveness of Strategies for Preventing Violence: Firearms Laws*, CDC, Task Force on Community Preventive Services, Oct 3, 2003 – a systematic review of 51 studies that evaluated the effects of selected firearms laws on violence
3. *Violent Encounters: A Study of Felonious Assaults on Our Nation's Law Enforcement Officers*, U.S. Department of Justice, August 2006
4. National Center for Health Statistics, Vital Statistics, Revised July 1999
5. Dr. Gary Kleck, University of Florida using FBI Uniform Crime Statistics, 1997
6. Dr. Gary Kleck, University of Florida using FBI Uniform Crime Statistics, 1997
7. *Index of Crime by State*, FBI Uniform Crime Reports (UCR) for 2000, p. 79, Table 5
8. FBI Uniform Crime Reports, September 15, 2000
9. FBI Uniform Crime Reports, September 15, 2000
10. *Under the Gun*, Wright, Rossi, Daly, University of Massachusetts, 1981
11. *Under the Gun*, Wright, Rossi, Daly, University of Massachusetts, 1981
12. *Under the Gun*, Wright, Rossi, Daly, University of Massachusetts, 1981
13. *Understanding Why Crime Fell in the 1990s*, Steven Levit, Journal of Economic Perspectives, Winter 2004
14. FBI Uniform Crime Reports for 1992 and 1997
15. *Firearm Use by Offenders*, Bureau of Justice Statistics, November 2001
16. *Enforcement of the Brady Act, 2006*, Regional Justice Information Service, study funded by Bureau of Justice Statistics, Office of Justice Programs, U.S. Department of Justice
17. Dr. Jens Ludwig, Dr. Philip J. Cook, Journal of the American Medical Association, August 2000
18. *Gun Licensing Leads to Increased Crime, Lost Lives*, Prof. John Lott, L.A. Times, Aug 23, 2000, based on both the FBI Uniform Crime Statistics for 1990s and the U.S. Justice Department Crime Victimization Survey
19. Portrait of America survey, August 2000
20. Center for Disease Control, WISQARS online Fatal Injury Reports,

2010
21. Transactional Records Access Clearinghouse (TRAC) at Syracuse University covering 1992 through 1998
22. General Accounting Office (GAO) 2000 audit of the National Instant Check System between 11/30/98 and 11/30/99. This stat needs to be tempered by the fact that many initial rejections were due to database errors – false positives – where the buyer was later approved.
23. Bureau of Justice Statistics, Federal Firearm Offenders and Background Checks for Firearm Transfers, June 4, 2000
24. U.S. Justice Department statistics, 1999
25. U.S. Justice Department statistics, 1999
26. Bureau of Justice Statistics, Federal Firearm Offenders and Background Checks for Firearm Transfers, June 4, 2000
27. General Accounting Office report on the Implementation of NICS, February 2000
28. General Accounting Office report on the Implementation of NICS, February 2000
29. United States Treasury and Justice Department Report, 1999
30. *Federal Firearm Offenders* report, Bureau of Justice Statistics, June 4, 2000 – firearm suspects declined for prosecution by U.S. attorneys … some of the reasons listed for not prosecuting known gun criminals include "minimal federal interest" and "DOJ/U.S. Attorney policy"
31. FBI Uniform Crime Statistics, 1999
32. BATF, 1999
33. *Suing Gun Manufacturers: Hazardous to Our Health*, Sterling Burnett, National Center for Policy Analysis, 1999
34. Taking Dr. Gary Kleck's estimate of 2.5 million gun defenses each year, divided by the FBI estimates of crimes committed with a firearm.
35. *Shooting in the dark: estimating the cost of firearm injuries*, Max W and Rice DP, Health Affairs, 1993
36. Compiled by Mothers Against Drunk Driving (MADD)
37. *The Financial Costs of Gun Violence*, Linda Gunderson, Annals of Internal Medicine, September 21, 1999
38. *Gun Violence: The Real Costs*, Ludwig, Cook, 2000
39. *Armed Resistance to Crime*, Kleck, Gertz, Journal of Criminal Law and Criminology, vol. 86, no. 1, 1995: 150
40. *Preventing Crime: What Works, What Doesn't, What's Promising*, National Institute of Justice, July 1998
41. Garen Wintemute, Violence Prevention Research Program, U.C., Davis, 1997
42. Jon Vernick, John Hopkins Center for Gun Policy and Research, Sacramento and St. Louis studies
43. District of Columbia buyback program, 1999

44. *Gun Policy & Law Enforcement survey*, PoliceOne, March 2013

45. David Kennedy, Senior Researcher, Harvard University Kennedy School Program in Criminal Justice, in appearance on Fox News, November 22, 2000

46. Christopher Koper of Pennsylvania's Jerry Lee Center of Criminology, reported in Criminology & Public Policy, American Society of Criminology, March 2002

47. Associated Press report, April 17, 2001

48. *Safe Storage Gun Laws: Accidental Deaths, Suicides, and Crime*, Prof. John Lott, Yale School of Law, March 2000

49. *Safe Storage Gun Laws: Accidental Deaths, Suicides, and Crime*, Prof. John Lott, Yale School of Law, March 2000

50. Sierra Times and various wire services, September 2000

51. This myth derives from *Firearm Death Rates and Association with Level of Firearm Purchase Background Check*, Steven A. Sumner, Layde, Guse, American Journal of Preventive Medicine, Volume 35, Issue 1, Pages 1-86 (July 2008)

Guns in Other Countries

Myth: Countries with strict gun control have less crime

Fact: In America, we can demonstrate that private ownership of guns reduces crime, but from country to country there is no correlation between gun availability and the violent crime rate. Consider this:

		Crime Rate	
		High	Low
Gun Availabilty	High	United States	Switzerland
	Low	Mexico	Japan

Or, to use detailed data, we can contrast the per capita homicide rate with the per capita gun ownership rate between different industrialized countries (see graph below). Contrasting the data shows zero correlation between the availability of guns and the overall homicide rate.

Fact: Countries with the strictest gun-control laws also tended to have the highest homicide rates.[1]

Fact: According to the U.N., as of 2005, Scotland was the most violent country in the developed world, with people three times more likely to be assaulted than in America. Violent crime there has doubled over the last 20 years. 3% of Scots had been victims of assault compared with 1.2% in America.[2]

Fact: "... the major surveys completed in the past 20 years or more provide no evidence of any relationship between the total number of legally held firearms in society and the rate of armed crime. Nor is there a relationship between the severity of controls imposed in various countries or the mass of bureaucracy involved with many control systems with the apparent ease of access to firearms by criminals and terrorists."[3]

Fact: Even if we examine just firearm ownership and firearm homicide by country, we see no correlation between the two.[4]

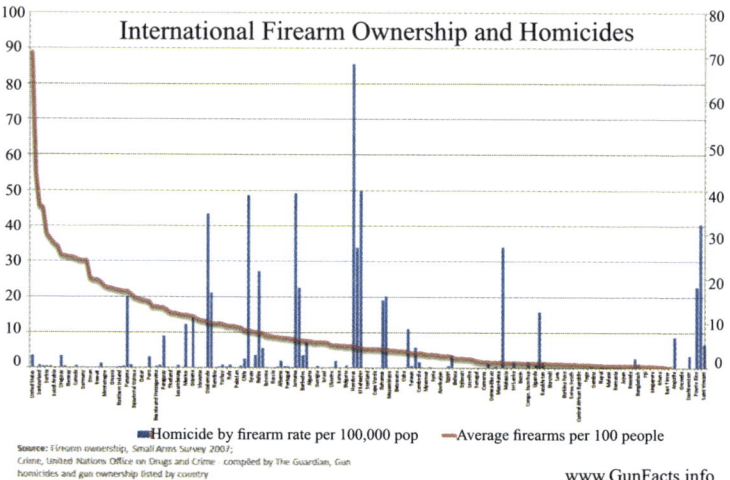

Fact: Switzerland has relatively lenient gun control for Europe[5], and has the third-lowest homicide rate of the top nine major European countries, and the same per capita rate as England and Wales.[6]

Fact: Indeed, the Swiss basically have a military rifle in nearly every closet. "Everybody who has served in the army is allowed to keep their personal weapon, even after the end of their military service."[7]

Fact: "We don't have as many guns [in Brazil] as the United States, but we use them more."[8] Brazil has mandatory licensing, registration, and maximum personal ownership quotas. It now bans any new sales to private citizens. Their homicide rate is almost three (3) times higher than the U.S.[9]

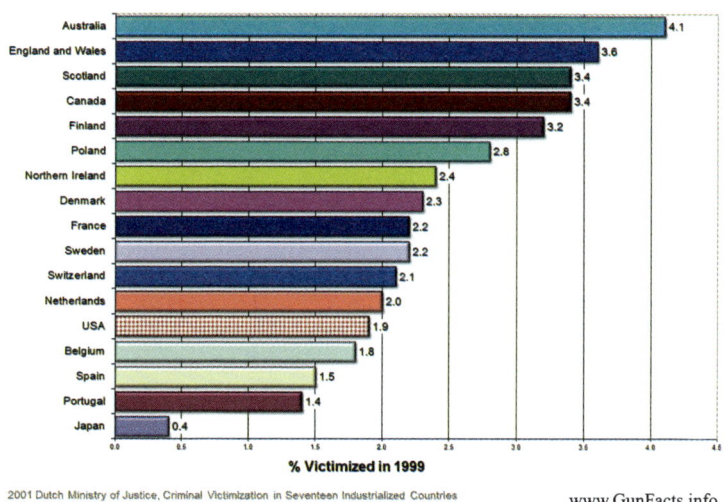

Contact Crime Victimization Rates

Country	% Victimized in 1999
Australia	4.1
England and Wales	3.6
Scotland	3.4
Canada	3.4
Finland	3.2
Poland	2.8
Northern Ireland	2.4
Denmark	2.3
France	2.2
Sweden	2.2
Switzerland	2.1
Netherlands	2.0
USA	1.9
Belgium	1.8
Spain	1.5
Portugal	1.4
Japan	0.4

2001 Dutch Ministry of Justice, Criminal Victimization in Seventeen Industrialized Countries   www.GunFacts.info

Fact: In Canada around 1920, before there was any form of gun control, their homicide rate was 7% of the U.S rate. By 1986, and after significant gun control legislation, Canada's homicide rate was 35% of the U.S. rate – a significant increase.[10] In 2003, Canada had a violent crime rate more than double that of the U.S. (963 vs. 475 per 100,000).[11]

Fact: One study of Canadian firearm law and homicide rates spanning 34 years "failed to demonstrate a beneficial association between legislation and firearm homicide rates" for three major gun control bills. [12]

Fact: Many of the countries with the strictest gun control have the highest rates of violent crime. Australia and England, which have virtually banned gun ownership, have the highest rates of robbery, sexual assault, and assault with force of the top 17 industrialized countries.[13]

Fact: The crime rate is 66% higher in four Canadian Prairie Provinces than in the northern US states across the border.[14]

Fact: Strict controls over existing arms failed in Finland. Despite needs-based licensing, storage laws and transportation restrictions,[15] Finland experienced a multiple killing school shooting in 2007.[16]

Myth: Britain has strict gun control and thus a low crime rate

Fact: The United Kingdom has *always* had a lower homicide rate than the United States, even when British citizens could legally buy machine guns (Briton's modern era of gun control did not ramp up until the 1960s). The difference is cultural, not legal.

Fact: Since gun banning has escalated in the UK, the rate of crime – especially violent crime – has risen.

Fact: Ironically, firearm use in crimes in the UK has ***doubled*** in the decade since handguns were banned.[17]

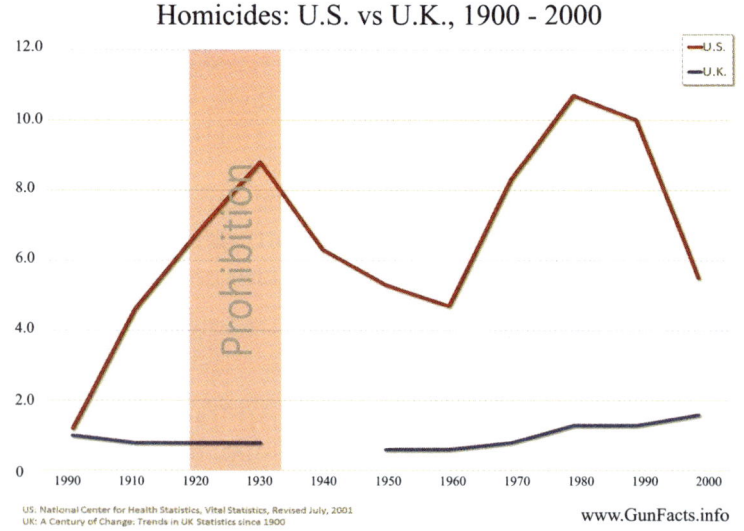

Homicides: U.S. vs U.K., 1900 - 2000

US: National Center for Health Statistics, Vital Statistics, Revised July, 2001
UK: A Century of Change: Trends in UK Statistics since 1900

www.GunFacts.info

Fact: Britain has the highest rate of violent crime in Europe, more so than the United States or even South Africa. They also have the second highest overall crime rate in the European Union. In 2008, Britain had a violent crime rate nearly five times higher than the United States (2034 vs. 446 per 100,000 population).[18]

Fact: 67% of British residents surveyed believe that "As a result of gun and knife crime [rising], the area I live in is not as safe as it was five years ago."[19]

Fact: U.K. street robberies soared 28% in 2001. Violent crime was up 11%, murders up 4%, and rapes were up 14%.[20]

Fact: This trend continued in the U.K in 2004 with a 10% increase in street crime, 8% increase in muggings, and a 22% increase in robberies.

Fact: In 1919, before it had any gun control, the U.K. had a homicide rate that was 8% of the U.S. rate. By 1986, and after enacting significant gun control, the rate was 9% – practically unchanged.[21]

Fact: "... [There is] nothing in the statistics for England and Wales to suggest that either the stricter controls on handguns prior to 1997 or the ban imposed since have controlled access to such firearms by criminals."[22]

Fact: Comparing crime rates between America and Britain is fundamentally flawed. In America, a gun crime is recorded as a gun crime. In Britain, a crime is only recorded when there is a final disposition (a conviction). All unsolved gun crimes in Britain are not reported as gun crimes, grossly undercounting the amount of gun crime there.[23] To make matters worse, British law enforcement has been exposed for falsifying criminal reports to create falsely lower crime figures, in part to preserve tourism.[24]

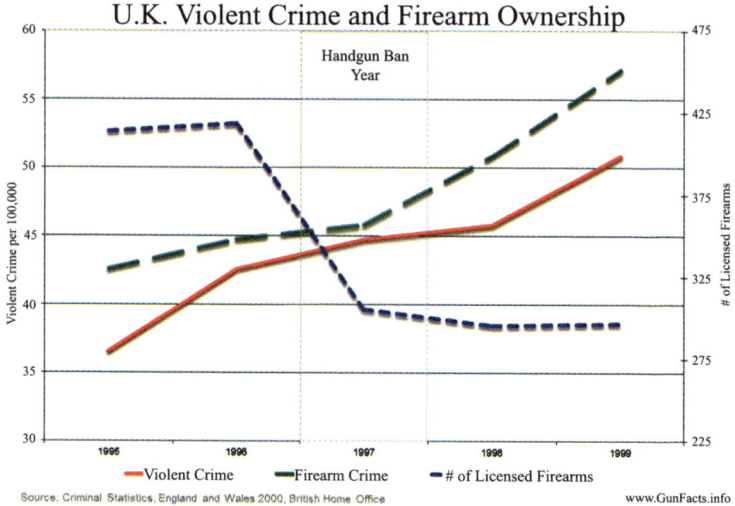

U.K. Violent Crime and Firearm Ownership

Handgun Ban Year

Violent Crime per 100,000

# of Licensed Firearms

- Violent Crime
- Firearm Crime
- # of Licensed Firearms

Source: Criminal Statistics, England and Wales 2000, British Home Office

www.GunFacts.info

Fact: An ongoing parliamentary inquiry in Britain into the growing number of black market weapons has concluded that there are more than three million illegally held firearms in circulation – double the number believed to have been held 10 years ago – and that criminals are more willing than ever to use them. One in three criminals under the age of 25 possesses or has access to a firearm.[25]

Fact: Handgun homicides in England and Wales reached an all-time high in 2000, years after a virtual ban on private handgun ownership. More than 3,000 crimes involving handguns were recorded in 1999-2000, including 42 homicides, 310 cases of attempted murder, 2,561 robberies and 204 burglaries.[26]

British Offenses in 2000	
Offense Category	**Increase From Pre-ban**
Armed Robbery	170.1%
Kidnapping/Abduction	144.0%
Assault	130.9%
Attempted Murder	117.6%
Sexual Assault	112.6%

Fact: Handguns were used in 3,685 British offenses in 2000 compared with 2,648 in 1997, an increase of 40%.[27] It is interesting to note:

- Of the 20 areas with the lowest number of legal firearms, 10 had an above average level of "gun crime."
- Of the 20 areas with the highest levels of legal guns, only 2 had armed crime levels above the average.

Fact: Between 1997 and 1999, there were 429 murders in London, the highest two-year figure for more than 10 years – nearly two-thirds of those involved firearms – in a country that has virtually banned private firearm ownership.[28]

Fact: Over the last century, the British crime rate was largely unchanged. In the late nineteenth century, the per capita homicide rate in Britain was between 1.0 and 1.5 per 100,000.[29] In the late twentieth century, after a near ban on gun ownership, the homicide rate is around 1.4.[30] This implies that the homicide rate did not vary with either the level of gun control or gun availability.

Fact: The U.K. has strict gun control and a rising homicide rate of 1.4 per 100,000. Switzerland has the highest per capita firearm ownership rate on the planet (all males age 20 to 42 are required to keep rifles or pistols at home) and has a homicide rate of 1.2 per 100,000. To date, there has never been a schoolyard massacre in Switzerland.[31]

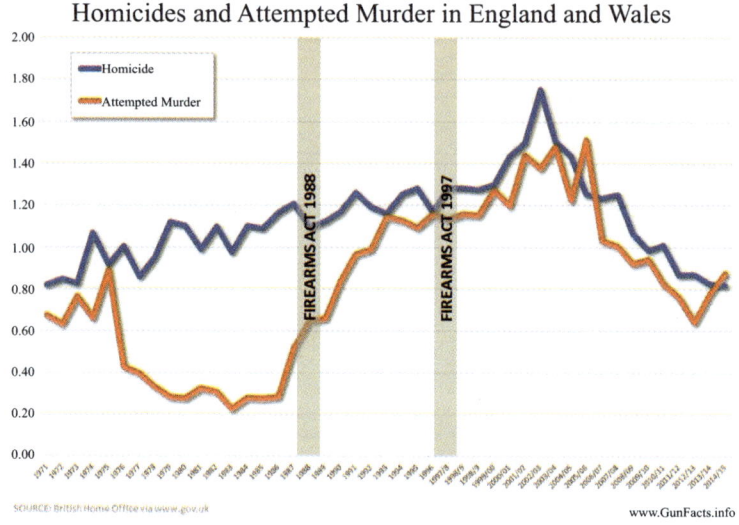

Homicides and Attempted Murder in England and Wales

SOURCE: British Home Office via www.gov.uk

www.GunFacts.info

Fact: "... the scale of gun crime in the capital [London] has forced senior officers to set up a specialist unit to deal with ... shootings."[32]

Myth: Gun control in Australia is curbing crime

Fact: Homicides were falling *before* the Australian firearm ban. In the seven years before and after the Australian ban, the rate of decline was identical (down to four decimal places). Homicides dropped steeply starting in 2003, but all of this decline was associated with non-firearm and non-knife murders (fewer beatings, poisonings, drownings, etc.).[33]

Fact: Crime has been rising since enacting a sweeping ban on private gun ownership. In the first two years after the ban, government statistics showed a dramatic increase in criminal activity.[34] In 2001-2002, homicides were up another 20%.[35] From the inception of firearm confiscation to March 27, 2000, the numbers are:

- Firearm-related murders were up 19%
- Armed robberies were up 69%
- Home invasions were up 21%

The sad part is that in the 15 years before the national gun confiscation:

- Firearm-related homicides dropped nearly 66%
- Firearm-related deaths fell 50%

Fact: Gun crimes have been rising throughout Australia since guns were banned. In Sydney alone, robbery rates with guns rose 160% in 2001, more than in the previous year.[36]

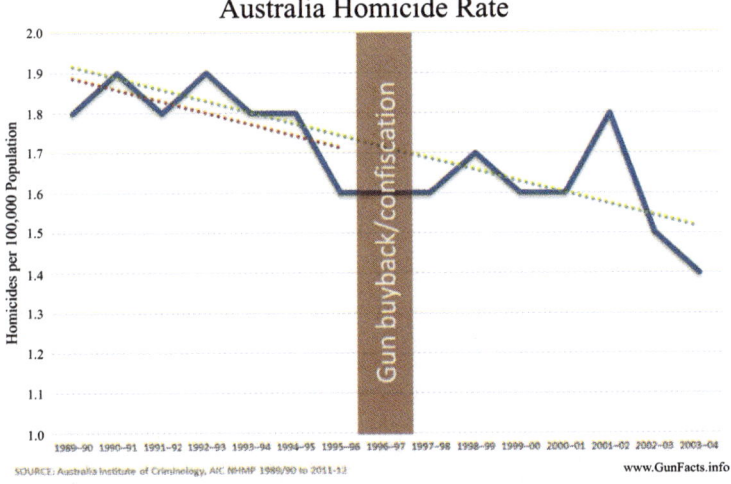

Australia Homicide Rate

Fact: A ten-year Australian study has concluded that firearm confiscation had no effect on crime rates.[37] A separate report also concluded that Australia's 1996 gun control laws "found

[no] evidence for an impact of the laws on the pre-existing decline in firearm homicides"[38] and yet another report from Australia for a similar time period indicates the same lack of decline in firearm homicides.[39]

Fact: Despite having much stricter gun control than New Zealand (including a near ban on handguns) firearm homicides in both countries track one another over 25 years, indicating that gun control is not a control variable.[40]

Myth: Japan has strict gun control and a less violent society

Fact: In Japan, the total murder rate is almost 1 per 100,000. In the U.S., there are about 3.2 murders per 100,000 people each year by weapons other than firearms.[41] *This means that even if firearms in the U.S. could be eliminated, the U.S. would still have three times the murder rate of the Japanese.*

Myth: Gun bans elsewhere work

Fact: Though illegal, side-street gun makers thrive in the Philippines, primarily hand crafting exact replicas of submachine guns, which are often the simplest type of gun to manufacture. Estimates are that almost half of all guns in the Philippines are illegal.[42]

Fact: Chinese police destroyed 113 illegal gun factories and shops in a three-month crackdown in 2006. Police seized 2,445 tons of explosives, 4.81 million detonators and 117,000 guns.[43]

Myth: The United States has the highest violence rate because of lax gun control

Fact: The top 100 countries for homicide do not include the U.S.[44] The top ten countries all have near or total firearm bans.

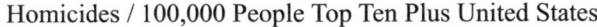
Homicides / 100,000 People Top Ten Plus United States

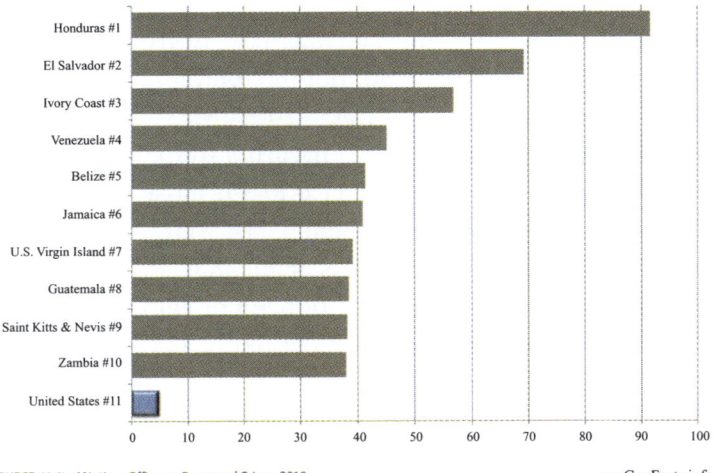

SOURCE: United Nations Office on Drugs and Crime, 2010   www.GunFacts.info

Myth: The U.S. has the highest rate of firearm deaths among 25 high-income countries

Fact: 60% of American "gun deaths" are suicides[45] and the U.S. has a suicide rate 11% higher[46] than international averages. This accounts for most of the difference.

Fact: The U.S. has a violent crime rate lower than 12 of 17 industrialized countries[47] due in large part to the 2.5 million annual defense gun uses.[48]

Myth: The United States is the source of 90% of drug syndicate guns in Mexico

Fact: This is an often-misquoted data point from the BATFE, who said 90% of the firearms that have been *interdicted in transport* to Mexico or recovered in Mexico came from the United States. Thus, the 90% number includes only the firearms American and Mexican police stop in transport.[49]

Fact: The original 90% number was derived from the number of firearms successfully traced, not the total number of firearms criminally used. For 2007-2008, Mexican officials recovered approximately 29,000 firearms from crime scenes and asked for BATFE traces of 11,000. Of those, the BATFE could trace roughly 6,000 of which 5,114 were confirmed to have come from the United States. Thus, 83% of the crime guns recovered in Mexico have not been or cannot be traced to America and the real number is most likely 17%.[50]

Fact: Mexican drug syndicates can buy guns anywhere. For the relatively under-powered civilian rifles coming from the United States, drug runners would pay between 300% and 400% above the market price. Thus, they can and are buying guns around the world.[51]

Fact: Mexican drug cartels – with $40 billion in annual revenues – have military armament that includes hand grenades, grenade launchers, armor-piercing munitions, antitank rockets and assault *rifles* smuggled in from Central American countries.[52] These are infantry weapons bought from around the world and not civilian rifles from the United States.

Myth: Mexico seizes 2,000 guns a day from the United States

Fact: The Mexican attorney general's office reports seizing a total of 29,000 weapons in all of 2007 and 2008, or about 14,500 weapons a year. And that is *all* types of weapons, regardless of country of origin.[53] Had they actually seized approximately 2,000 weapons per day, the total number of seized guns would be closer to 1,460,000.

Myth: Thousands of guns go into Mexico from the U.S. every day

Fact: In Senate Committee testimony, the BAFTE said the number was likely at worst to be in the "hundreds".[54] As evidenced above, for 2007 and 2008, the average for all firearms seizures was closer to 40 per day (29,000 guns/730 days), and only a fraction of these came from the USA by any means.

1. *Violence, Guns and Drugs: A Cross-Country Analysis*, Jeffery A. Miron, Department of Economics, Boston University, University of Chicago Press Journal of Law & Economics, October 2001
2. *Scotland tops list of world's most violent countries*, The Times, September 19, 2005
3. *Minutes of Evidence*, Colin Greenwood, Select Committee on Northern Ireland Affairs, January 29, 2003
4. Firearm ownership, Small Arms Survey 2007; Crime, United Nations Office on Drugs and Crime - compiled by The Guardian, *Gun homicides and gun ownership listed by country*
5. In Switzerland, handguns are obtainable once a person obtains a simple police permit which is valid for six months. *Federal law over weapons, weapon accessories and ammunition (weapon law, WG)*, Federal Assembly of the Swiss Confederation, May 2007
6. Carol Kalish, International Crime Rates, Bureau of Justice Statistics Special Report (Washington: Department of Justice, May 1988). 1984 data for Switzerland, and the 1983 data for England and Wales.
7. *Army rifles remain racked at home*, Swiss Defense Ministry statement, May 15, 2004
8. *Chocolates for guns? Brazil targets gun violence*, Rubem César Fernandes, executive secretary of Viva Rio, a nongovernmental agency that studies urban crime, Christian Science Monitor, August 10, 1999
9. *Homicide trends in the United States*, U.S. data: Bureau of Justice Statistics, September 2004. Brazil data: Nations Educational, Scientific and Cultural Organization, 2005.
10. *Targeting Guns*, Gary Kleck, Aldine Transaction, 1997, at 360
11. Juristat: Crime Statistics in Canada, 2004 and FBI Uniform Crime Statistics online
12. *Canadian Firearms Legislation and Effects on Homicide 1974 to 2008*,

Caillin Langmann, Journal of Interpersonal Violence, September 30, 2011

13. *Criminal Victimization in Seventeen Industrialized Countries*, Dutch Ministry of Justice, 2001

14. *A Comparison of Violent and Firearm Crime Rates in the Canadian Prairie Provinces and Four U.S. Border States, 1961-2003*, Parliamentary Research Branch of the Library of Parliament, March 7, 2005

15. *National Report by Finland*, United Nations Office for Disarmament Affairs

16. Pekka-Eric Auvinen shooting in Tuusula, Finland on November 8, 2007

17. *Weapons sell for just £50 as suspects and victims grow ever younger*, The Times, August 24, 2007

18. *The most violent country in Europe: Britain is also worse than South Africa and U.S.*, Daily Mail, July 3, 2009, citing a joint report of the European Commission and United Nations

19. YouGov survey of 2,156 residents in Sept 2007

20. British Home Office, reported by BBC news, July 12, 2002

21. *Targeting Guns*, Gary Kleck, Aldine Transaction, 1997, at 359

22. *Minutes of Evidence*, Colin Greenwood, Select Committee on Northern Ireland Affairs, January 29, 2003

23. *Fear in Britain*, Gallant, Hills, Kopel, Independence Institute, July 18, 2000

24. *Crime Figures a Sham, Say Police*, Daily Telegraph, April 1, 1996

25. Reported in The Guardian, September 3, 2000

26. *42 killed by handguns last year*, The Times, January 10, 2001, reporting on statistics supplied by the British Home Office

27. *Illegal Firearms in the UK*, Centre for Defense Studies at King's College in London, July 2001

28. *Illegal Firearms in the UK*, Centre for Defense Studies at King's College in London, July 2001

29. *Crime and Society in England 1750-1900*, Clive Emsley, 1987, at 36

30. *Where Kids and Guns Do Mix*, Stephen P. Halbrook, Wall Street Journal, June 1999

31. *Where Kids and Guns Do Mix*, Stephen P. Halbrook, Wall Street Journal, June 1999

32. Associated News Media, April 30, 2001

33. Australia Institute of Criminology, AIC NHMP 1989/90 to 2011-12

34. *Crime and Justice - Crimes Recorded by Police*, Australian Bureau of Statistics, 2000

35. *Report #46: Homicide in Australia, 2001-2002*, Australian Institute of Criminology, April 2003

36. *Costa targets armed robbers*, The Sydney Morning Herald, April 4, 2002

37. *Gun Laws and Sudden Death: Did the Australian Firearms Legislation of 1996 Make a Difference?* Dr. Jeanine Baker and Dr. Samara McPhedran, British Journal of Criminology, November 2006.

38. *Austrian firearms: data require cautious approach*, S. McPhedran, S. McPhedran, and J. Baker, The British Journal of Psychiatry, 2007, 191:562

39. *Australian firearms legislation and unintentional firearm deaths a theoretical explanation for the absence of decline following the 1996 gun laws Public Health*, Samara McPhedran, Jeanine Baker, Public Health, Volume 122, Issue 3

40. *Firearm Homicide in Australia, Canada, and New Zealand: What Can We Learn from Long- Term International Comparisons?* Samara McPhedran, Jeanine Baker, and Pooja Singh, Journal of Interpersonal Violence, March 16, 2010

41. Japan data: *1996 Demographic Yearbook*, United Nations, 1998; US data: FBI Uniform Crime Statistics, 1996.

42. *Filipino gunsmiths are making a killing*, Taipei Times, May 7, 2005

43. China Radio International Online, September 7, 2006

44. SOURCE: United Nations Office on Drugs and Crime, 2010

45. Center for Disease Control WISQARS Fatal Injury Data is the National Vital Statistics System for 2010

46. World Health Organization, mortality database as of November 2006

47. *Criminal Victimization in Seventeen Industrialized Countries*, Dutch Ministry of Justice, 2001

48. *Targeting Guns*, Gary Kleck, Aldine Transaction, 1997

49. *Mexico's Massive Illegal weapons coming from China and the U.S.*, American Chronicle, March 14, 2009

50. *The Myth of 90 Percent*, Fox News, April 2, 2009, BATFE data distilled by William La Jeunesse and Maxim Lott

51. *Southwest Border Region--Drug Transportation and Homeland Security Issues*, National Drug Intelligence Center, October 2007

52. *Drug cartels' new weaponry means war*, Los Angeles Times, March 15, 2009

53. *The Myth of 90 Percent*, William La Jeunesse and Maxim Lott, Fox News, April 2, 2009

54. Senate Committee Judiciary, William Hoover, Assistant Director, Bureau of Alcohol, Tobacco, & Firearms, March 17, 2009

Licensing and Registration

Myth: Other countries register guns to fight crime

Fact: In these countries, non-registration rates (people keeping guns without registering them) are high, ranging from 22% as many unregistered as registered (Australia) to 1,500% as many unregistered (Greece).[1]

Fact: Most of these laws were enacted in the post-World War I period to prevent civil uprisings as had occurred in Russia. A report of "Committee on the Control of Firearms," written by British Home Office officials in 1918, was the basis for registration in the U.K., Australia, Canada, and New Zealand.[2]

Fact: Although restrictions were few in the United States and the number of legally held handguns exceeded those on the Canadian side by a factor of ten, rates of homicide were virtually identical.[3]

Fact: Even so, registration does not prevent gun crimes. In a one week period, a licensed gun owner killed 12 people in England[4] and a Chinese security guard killed three judges in a court building[5] despite complete licensing and registration

Myth: Gun registration works

Fact: Internationally, there is no correlation between registration rates, percent of unregistered weapons, and homicide rates.[6]

Fact: Not in California. California has had handgun registration since 1909[7] and it has not had any impact on violent crime rates.[8]

Fact: Not in New Zealand. They repealed their gun registration law in the 1980s after police acknowledged its worthlessness.[9]

Fact: Not in Australia. One report states, "It seems just to be an elaborate system of arithmetic with no tangible aim. Probably, and with the best of intentions, it may have been thought that if it were known what firearms each individual in Victoria owned, some form of control may be exercised, and those who were guilty of criminal misuse could be readily identified. This is a fallacy, and has been proven not to be the case."[10] In addition, cost to Australian taxpayers exceeded $200 million annually.[11]

Fact: Not in Canada. More than 20,000 Canadian gun-owners have publicly refused to register their firearms. Many others (as many as 300,000[12]) are silently ignoring the law.

- The provincial governments of Alberta, Saskatchewan, and Manitoba have dumped both the administration and the enforcement of all federal gun-control laws right back into Ottawa's lap, throwing the Canadian government into a paper civil war.

- And all at a cost more than 1,646% the original projected cost[13] (the original cost was estimated at 5% of all police expenditures in Canada[14]). "The gun registry as it sits right now is causing law abiding citizens to register their guns but it does nothing to take one illegal gun off the street or to increase any type of penalty for anybody that violates any part of the legislation," according to Al Koenig, President, Calgary Police Association.[15] "We have an ongoing gun crisis, including firearms-related homicides lately in Toronto, and a law registering firearms has neither deterred these crimes nor helped us solve any of them," according to Toronto police Chief Julian Fantino.[16]

- The system was so bad that six Canadian provinces (British Columbia, Manitoba, Saskatchewan, Alberta,

Nova Scotia, and Ontario) are refusing to prosecute firearm owners who fail to register.[17]

- A bill to abolish the registry has been tabled (introduced) in the Canadian Parliament, which if passed, would eliminate the registry completely.[18]

- A Saskatchewan MP who endorsed the long gun registry when first proposed has introduced legislation to abolish it stating that, "[the registry] has not saved one life in Canada, and it has been a financial sinkhole … absolutely useless in helping locate the 255,000 people who have been prohibited from owning firearms by the courts."[19]

- In April 2012, the Canadian long gun registry was terminated.

Fact: Not in Germany. The Federal Republic of Germany began comprehensive gun registration in 1972. The government estimated that between 17,000,000 and 20,000,000 guns were to be registered, but only 3,200,000 surfaced, leaving 80% unaccounted for.[20]

Fact: Not in Boston, Cleveland, or California. These cities and state require registration of "assault weapons." The compliance rate in Boston and Cleveland is about 1%.[21]

Fact: Criminals don't register their guns, nor are they legally required to do so.[22]

Myth: Gun registration will help police find suspects

Fact: Registration is required in Hawaii, Chicago and Washington DC. Yet there has not been a single case where registration was instrumental in identifying someone who committed a crime.[23] Criminals very rarely leave their guns at the scene of the crime. Would-be criminals also virtually never get licenses or register their weapons.

Fact: It may cause police to shoot citizens unnecessarily. "My research into more than a dozen raids that turned out badly is that … the presence of a firearm wires officers into a much higher tendency to shoot. [T]he presence of a legally possessed firearm bought to protect the home may get totally innocent people killed by the police who casually use SWAT for drug search warrants especially if they register."[24]

Myth: Registration does not lead to confiscation

Fact: It did in Canada. The handgun registration law of 1934 was the source used to identify and confiscate (without compensation) over half of the registered handguns in 2001.[25]

Fact: It did in Germany. The 1928 Law on Firearms and Ammunition (before the Nazis came into power) required all firearms to be registered. When Hitler came into power, the existing lists were used for confiscating weapons.

Fact: It did in Australia. In 1996, the Australian government confiscated over 660,000 previously legal weapons from their citizens.

Fact: It did in California. The 1989 Roberti-Roos Assault Weapons Control Act required registration. Due to shifting definitions of "assault weapons," many legal firearms are now being confiscated by the California government.

Fact: It did in New York City. In 1967, New York City passed an ordinance requiring a citizen to obtain a permit to own a rifle or shotgun, which would then be registered. In 1991, the city passed a ban on the private possession of some semi-automatic rifles and shotguns, and "registered" owners were told that those firearms had to be surrendered, rendered inoperable, or taken out of the city.

Fact: It did in Bermuda, Cuba, Greece, Ireland, Jamaica, and Soviet Georgia as well.

Myth: Licensing will keep bad people from obtaining or using guns

Fact: Not in Canada. Canadian homicide rates were virtually unchanged before and after gun registration requirements were implemented (151 per 100,000 people in 1998 and 149 per 100,000 in 2002).[26]

Fact: In New York State alone, approximately 100,000 persons are convicted of unlicensed operation of a motor vehicle each year, and this is probably a small proportion of the actual number of people who drive without a valid license.[27] Licensing requirements don't stop ineligible people from driving, and they do not stop ineligible people from acquiring guns.

Fact: As long as the unlicensed purchaser is never caught with the handgun, the unlawful sale will go unnoticed. The risk of detection is negligible. If the unlicensed handgun owner is arrested, he could claim that he did not need a license because he had owned this handgun before licensing went into effect.[28]

Fact: Currently, federal prosecutors do not eagerly accept felon-in-possession cases for prosecution unless the felon is a hardened criminal who represents a threat to the public.[29]

Fact: According to the Supreme Court, criminals do not have to obtain licenses or register their weapons, as that would be an act of self-incrimination.[30]

Fact: Prohibition (which started as a 'moderation' movement) didn't keep people from drinking. Instead it turned millions of otherwise honest and sober citizens into criminals, overnight.

Fact: Most police do not see the benefit. "It is my belief that [licensing and registration] significantly misses the mark because it diverts our attention from what should be our common goal: holding the true criminals accountable for the crimes they commit and getting them off the street."[31]

Fact: In 2005, agencies reported 1,400 arrests of persons denied a firearm or permit; but the U.S. Department of Justice accepted only 135 of those denial cases for prosecution.[32] Given the poor performance of the Federal government in prosecuting felons identified by an instant background check trying to buy firearms, there is little to support firearm licensing as a crime prevention measure.

Myth: Guns from the U.S. create crime in other countries

Fact: Canada, which shares the longest and most open border with the U.S., doesn't think so, saying that guns from the U.S. are a "small part" of the problem.[33]

Myth: Guns should be registered and licensed like cars

Fact: You do not need a license to buy a car. You can buy as many as you want and drive them all you like on your own property without a license.

Fact: Cars are registered because they are (a) sources of tax revenue, (b) objects of fraud in some transactions, and (c) significant theft targets. Thus, we ask the government to track them.

Fact: There is no constitutionally guaranteed right to keep and bear automobiles, and thus they are subject to greater regulation than guns.

Fact: There are more guns in the U.S. than cars (228,000,000 guns and 207,754,000 automobiles). Yet you are 31 times more likely to be accidentally killed by a car than a gun according to the National Safety Council[34] ... despite cars having been registered and licensed for almost 100 years.

1. *Small Arms Survey*, 2003
2. *Response to Philip Alpers' submission to the California State Assembly Select Committee on Gun Violence*, Steven W. Kendrick, January 2000
3. *Homicide and the Prevalence of Handguns: Canada and the United States*, 1976 to 1980, American Journal of Epidemiology, Brandon Centrewall, Volume 134, December 1991. Though the rate of homicides as a whole were different, when demographics between the two cities were equalized, the homicide rates matched.
4. *Gun control and ownership laws in the UK*, BBC, June 3, 2010
5. *Man shoots dead three judges in China court*, Bangkok Post, June 1, 2010
6. *Small Arms Survey*, 2003 for registration rates, *United Nations Office on Drugs and Crime*, for homicide statistics
7. In conversation between the author of *Gun Facts* and a representative of California Department of Justice.
8. FBI, Uniform Crime Reports, via the *Data Online* data analysis tool on the website of the Bureau of Justice Statistics.
9. Background to the Introduction of Firearms User Licensing Instead of Rifle and Shotgun Registration Under the Arms Act 1983 (Wellington, New Zealand: n.p., 1983)
10. Registration Firearms System, Chief Inspector Newgreen, CRB File 39-1-1385/84
11. *The Failed Experiment: Gun Control and Public Safety in Canada, Australia, England and Wales,* Gary Mauser, The Fraser Institute, 2003
12. Standing Committee on Justice and Human Rights, Evidence number 55, June 5, 2003
13. *Ottawa Under Pressure Over Gun Registry Fiasco,* David Ljunggren, Reuters, December 4, 2002
14. *When 'Gun Control' costs lives,* John Lott, Firing Line, September 2001
15. Calgary Herald, September 1, 2000
16. *Opponents increase pressure to halt Canada's gun control program,* Associated Press, Jan 3, 2002
17. *Victoria won't enforce firearms act,* Vancouver Sun, June 06, 2003

18. *An Act to amend the Criminal Code and the Firearms Act,* received first reading June 19, 2006

19. *$2 billion worth of police will save more lives than one gun registry,* Garry Breitkreuz, National Post, February 27, 2009

20. *Why Gun Registration Will Fail,* Ted Drane, Australian Shooters Journal, May 1997

21. *The Samurai, the Mountie, and the Cowboy: Should America Adopt the Gun Controls of Other Democracies,* David B. Kopel, 231, n.210 (1992)

22. Haynes vs. U.S. 390 U.S. 85, 1968. The Supreme Court concluded that forcing a criminal to register their illegal guns was a form of self-incrimination.

23. *Gun Licensing Leads to Increased Crime, Lost Lives,* John Lott, L.A. Times, Aug 23, 2000

24. Joseph McNamara, former San Jose, California police chief, fellow at Stanford University's Hoover Institution quoted in *California Gun Law Paves the Way for Confiscation,* Reason, January 2014

25. *Civil Disobedience in Canada: It Just Happened to Be Guns,* Dr. Paul Gallant, and Dr. Joanne Eisen, Idaho Observer, August 2000

26. Statistics Canada, Oct 1, 2003

27. Journal of Criminal Law and Criminology, Northwestern University School of Law, 1998

28. Journal of Criminal Law and Criminology, Northwestern University School of Law, 1998

29. *Old Chief V. United States: Stipulating Away Prosecutorial Accountability,* Daniel C. Richman, 83 Va. L. Rev. 939, 982-85 (1997)

30. Haynes vs. U.S. 390 U.S. 85, 1968

31. *When 'Gun Control' costs lives,* Bob Brooks, Firing Line, September 2001

32. *Background Checks for Firearm Transfers 2005,* U.S. Department of Justice, Office of Justice Programs, November 2006

33. Globe and Mail, Paul Culver, August 15, 2005

34. Automobiles estimates: Federal Highway Administration, October 1998. Firearm estimates: FBI Uniform Crime Statistics, 1996.

Police and Guns

Myth: More police officers are killed on duty in states with more guns

Fact: Police homicide rates are so low that statistical analysis begs inaccuracies due to the rareness of such killings. Using the study that made this claim[1] the rate of civilian homicides was 60 times that of police officers, using the *highest* rate of police homicides.[2] To give you an idea of how small the numbers are, a mere 47 officers were killed with guns in 2014 (excluding firearm accidents).[3] Thus, the researchers were attempting to compare police homicides for each state when, on average, there was less than one such homicide per state.

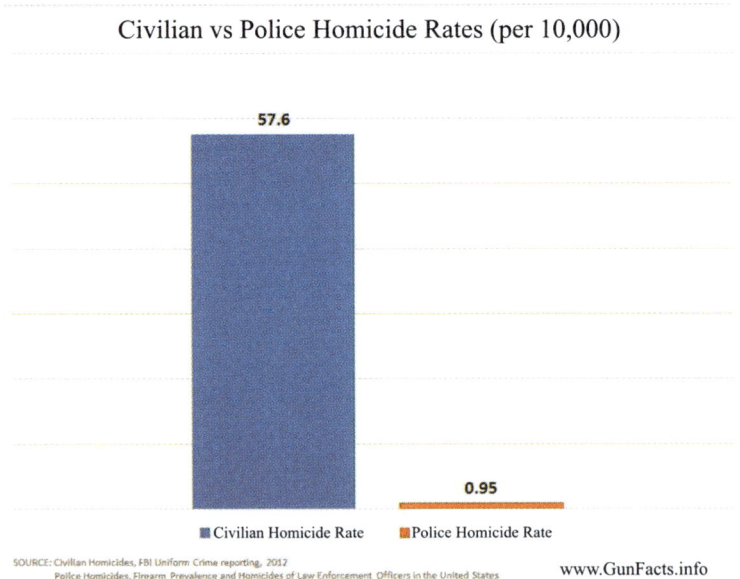

Civilian vs Police Homicide Rates (per 10,000)

57.6

0.95

■ Civilian Homicide Rate   ■ Police Homicide Rate

SOURCE: Civilian Homicides, FBI Uniform Crime reporting, 2012
Police Homicides, Firearm Prevalence and Homicides of Law Enforcement Officers in the United States

www.GunFacts.info

Myth: Police favor gun control

Fact: The National Association of Chiefs of Police polled its members[4] and determined that:

- 86% want nationwide reciprocity for concealed carry licensees.
- 76% think armed citizen can help cops reduce violent crime.
- 88% believe any vetted (non-criminal) citizen should be able to buy a gun.

Fact: 94% of law enforcement officials believe that citizens should be able to purchase firearms for self-defense and sporting purposes.[5]

Fact: In a survey of 15,000 law enforcement professionals:[6]
- 96% opposed limiting magazine capacity
- 91% think banning "assault weapons" would have no effect or a negative effect
- 62% said they would not enforce new gun control laws

Fact: 65.8% believe there should be no gun rationing, such as 'one gun per month' schemes.

Fact: 97.9% of police officers believe criminals are able to obtain any type of firearm through illegal means.

Fact: "Gun control has not worked in D.C. The only people who have guns are criminals. We have the strictest gun laws in the nation and one of the highest murder rates. It's quicker to pull your Smith & Wesson than to dial 911 if you're being robbed."[7]

Myth: Police are our protection — people don't need guns

Fact: Tell that to 14,196 murder victims, 345,031 robbery victims, and 79,770 rape victims who the police could not help.[8]

Fact: The courts have consistently ruled that the police do not have an obligation to protect individuals. In Warren V.

District of Columbia Metropolitan Police Department, 444
A.2d 1 (D.C. App. 1981), the court stated "… courts have
without exception concluded that when a municipality or other
governmental entity undertakes to furnish police services, it
assumes a duty only to the public at large and not to individual
members of the community."

Fact: There are not enough police to protect everyone. In
1999, there were about 150,000 police officers on duty at any
one time.[9]

- This is on-duty police. This includes desk clerks,
  command sergeants, etc. – far fewer than 150,000 cops
  are cruising your neighborhood.
- There were approximately 271,933,702 people living in
  the United States in 1999.[10]
- Thus there is only one on-duty cop for every 1,813
  citizens!

Fact: Former Florida Attorney General Jim Smith told Florida
legislators that police responded to only 200,000 of 700,000
calls for help to Dade County authorities.

Fact: The United States Department of Justice found that, in
1989, there were 168,881 crimes of violence for which police
had not responded within 1 hour.

Fact: 95% of the time police arrived too late to prevent a
crime or arrest the suspect.[11]

Fact: 75% of protective/restraining orders are violated and
police often won't enforce them unless they witness the
violation.[12]

Fact: Despite prompt law enforcement responses, most armed
and violent attacks at schools were stopped by means other
than law enforcement intervention.[13] Often these interventions
were by administrators, teachers, or other students who were
licensed to carry firearms.

Myth: The supply of guns is a danger to law enforcement

Fact: The courts kill cops by letting felons out of prison early. Of police killed in the line of duty:

- 70% are killed by criminals with prior arrest records
- 53% of these criminals have prior convictions
- 22% are on probation when the officer is killed

Myth: "Cop Killer" bullets need to be banned

Fact: KTW rounds, wrongly labeled as "cop killer" bullets, were designed by police officers[14], for use by police to penetrate hard targets like car windshields. KTWs have never been sold to the general public.[15]

Myth: Teflon bullets are designed to penetrate police bullet-proof vests

Fact: KTW rounds are Teflon coated to prevent heat build-up in a police officer's gun barrel, not to pierce body armor.[16]

1. Firearm Prevalence and Homicides of Law Enforcement Officers in the United States, Swedler, Simmons, Dominici, and Hemenway, American Journal of Public Health, October 2015
2. Using the average national civilian homicide covering the period of their study for police.
3. Officer Down Memorial Page
4. 28th Annual National Survey Results, National Association of Chiefs of Police, 2016
5. 17th Annual National Survey of Police Chiefs & Sheriffs, National Association of Chiefs of Police, 2005
6. Gun Policy & Law Enforcement survey, PoliceOne, March 2013
7. Lt. Lowell Duckett, Special Assistant to DC Police Chief; President, Black Police Caucus, The Washington Post, March 22, 1996
8. FBI Uniform Crime Statistics, 2014

9. US Justice Department, 1998

10. US Census Bureau, 1999 estimate

11. This is 911 ... please hold, Witkin, Gordon, Guttman, Monika and Lenzy, Tracy. U.S. News & World Report, June 17, 1998

12. Anti-stalking laws usually are unable to protect targets, Ellen Sorokin, Washington Times, April 16, 2000

13. Threat Assessment in Schools, U.S. Secret Service and U.S. Department of Education, 2002

14. Developed by Daniel Turcos (a police sergeant) and Donald Ward (Dr. Kopsch's special investigator)

15. Cop Killer Bullets, Mike Casey, July 2000

16. Cop Killer Bullets, Mike Casey, July 2000

.50 Caliber Rifles

Myth: .50-calibers are the favorite weapon of terrorists

Fact: Most terrorist attacks are in the form of bombings (90%). Other acts, such as kidnapping (6%), armed attack (2%), arson (1%), firebombing (1%), and other methods (2%), are far less common.[1] Of the "armed attacks," the most common weapons used are fully-automatic AK-47 rifles.

Fact: A single .50 caliber rifle costs upwards of $10,000, yet terrorists can buy the favored AK-47 in Pakistan for less than $200. History shows they opt for the AK-47.

Fact: .50-caliber rifles are heavy (20-35 pounds), expensive (from $3,000 to $10,000 each, with ammunition costing $2-$5 for each round), impossible to conceal (typically four feet long), usually single shot (slow to reload), and impractical for terrorists.

Fact: .50-caliber rifles have only been used in 18 crimes in the history of the United States. [2]

Myth: American gun makers sold .50-calibers to terrorists

Fact: This "study" by the anti-gun Violence Policy Center was inaccurate. The rifles in question were sold to the United States government. Years later, the U.S. government gave the rifles to Afghan freedom fighters to defeat the former Soviet Union. There is no direct connection between gun makers and terrorists, and none of the rifles have been used in terrorist actions.[3]

Myth: .50-caliber shooters are terrorists in training

Fact: The average .50-caliber enthusiast is a successful businessman with an annual income of $50,000 or more – hardly a terrorist profile.[4]

Myth: The Founding Fathers would have had no use for a .50-caliber rifle

Fact: Common guns of the early American republic were larger than .50-caliber, many measuring up to .812 caliber. The famous Kentucky Rifle (a name eventually given to most rifles made by German immigrants) was usually between .60 to .75-caliber.

Myth: .50-calibers are capable of piercing airline fuel tanks from a mile away

Fact: Most expert long-distance shooters cannot hit a stationary target under perfect, windless conditions at such distances (one notable exception in Vietnam[5]). Ill-trained terrorists shooting a high-recoil .50-caliber rifle at fast moving targets – a 280 mph airplane – have no chance.

Fact: The only known uses of .50-caliber weapons in downing aircraft have been military aircraft using *fully-automatic machine guns* spraying fire while in combat against other aircraft, and as sniper fire on *stationary aircraft* (i.e., on the ground) on enemy airfields. Not even the military's best sharp shooters are going to ignite a jet's fuel tank when the jet is flying between 200-300 miles per hour.

Myth: .50-caliber bullets can penetrate concrete bunkers

Fact: "It takes 300 rounds to penetrate 2 meters of reinforced concrete at 100 meters."[6] At $5 per round, it would cost a terrorist $1,500 in ammunition to shoot into one bunker.

Myth: .50-caliber bullets can pierce light armor at 4 miles[7]

Fact: "At 35 meters distance [0.5% of the mythical "four mile" distance], a .50-caliber round will go through one inch armor plate."[8] Piercing any armor at four miles is highly improbable.

Fact: "It is exceedingly difficult to hit a target, even a large one … at anything over 1200 to 1500 yards by even highly trained individuals ... The ammo is designed for a machine gun, and is generally only good for 2-3 minute of angle [fraction of a degree] of accuracy. That equates to a 30-45 inch circle at 1500 yards with a perfect rifle, no wind or other conditions and a trained shooter."[9]

Myth: .50-caliber rifles can knock a helicopter from the sky

Fact: The terminal energy of a .50-caliber (6,000 ft-lbs) is not enough to knock a modern military aircraft from the sky unless it hits a critical component like a fuel line. Records exist showing this has been done with common, smaller caliber assault rifles such as AK-47s.

Myth: .50-caliber guns are for snipers

Fact: Americans have been long-distance target shooters since revolutionary times. According to period writings,

Americans were shooting small targets at upwards of 150 yards using simple Kentucky long rifles and muskets.[10]

Fact: "The use of [.50-caliber] by the IRA in Northern Ireland to shoot both soldiers and police officers at very short range (never more than 275 yards) also gave the weapon a worldwide notoriety when the world›s media slapped a 'sniper' label on the terrorists taking the shots. They obviously were not and soon ran scared when professional snipers were deployed to stop them."[11]

1. Facts and Figures About Terrorism, Dexter Ingram, Heritage Foundation, September 14, 2001 (some attacks had multiple methods which accounts for a total in excess of 100%).

2. Weaponry: .50 Caliber Rifle Crime, General Accounting Office Report number OSI-99-15R, revised Oct. 21, 2001.

3. Barret Manufacturing letter on their web site available January 12, 2001. This was confirmed during a visit by the BATF according to Dave Kopel in a National Review article "Guns and (Character) Assassination", December 21, 2001.

4. John Burtt, Fifty Caliber Shooters Policy Institute, Congressional testimony

5. One Shot, One Kill: American Combat Snipers in World War II, Korea, Vietnam, Beirut, C. Sasser and C. Roberts, Pocket Books, referring to Marine sniper Carlos Hathcock.

6. An Infantryman's Guide to Combat in Built-up Area, field manual 90-10-1, US Army, May 1993.

7. Senator Dianne Feinstein, Senate testimony, March 9, 2001.

8. An Infantryman's Guide to Combat in Built-up Area, field manual 90-10-1, US Army, May 1993.

9. An Infantryman's Guide to Combat in Built-up Area, field manual 90-10-1, US Army, May 1993.

10. Firearms Ownership & Manufacturing in Early America, Clayton Cramer, unpublished.

11. Sniper, Mark Spicer, Salamander Books, 2001.

Ballistic Fingerprinting

Myth: Every firearm leaves a unique "fingerprint" that can pinpoint the firearm used

Fact: A group of National Research Council scientists concluded that this has not yet been fully demonstrated. Their research suggests that the current technology for collecting and comparing images may not reliably distinguish very fine differences.[1]

Fact: "Firearms that generate markings on cartridge casings can change with use and can also be readily altered by the users. They are not permanently defined like fingerprints or DNA."[2]

Fact: "Automated computer matching systems do not provide conclusive results."[3]

Fact: "Because bullets are severely damaged on impact, they can only be examined manually".[4]

Fact: "Not all firearms generate markings on cartridge casings that can be identified back to the firearm."[5]

Fact: The same gun will produce different markings on bullets and casings, and different guns can produce similar markings.[6] Additionally, the type of ammunition actually used in a crime could differ from the type used when the gun was originally test-fired -- a difference that could lead to significant error in suggesting possible matches.[7]

Fact: The rifle used in the Martin Luther King assassination was test fired 18 times under court supervision, and the results showed that no two bullets were marked alike.[8] "Every test bullet was different because it was going over plating created by the previous bullet."

Fact: "The common layman seems to believe that two bullets fired from the same weapon are identical, down to the very last striation placed on them by the weapon. The trained firearms examiner knows how far that is from reality."[9]

Myth: A database of ballistic profiles will allow police to trace gun crimes

Fact: The National Research Council deemed a national ballistics database as impractical due to practical limitations of current technology for generating and comparing images of ballistic markings.[10]

Fact: Maryland's ballistics database "is not doing anything"[11] and "has not met the mission statement of the state police."[12] In the first five years of implementation, it failed to lead to any criminal arrest or convictions, despite collecting over 80,000 specimens at a cost of $2,567,633.[13]

Fact: More than 70% of armed career criminals get their guns from "off-the-street sales" and "criminal acts" such as burglaries[14], and 71% of these firearms are stolen.[15] Tracing these firearms will not lead to the criminals, as the trail stops at the last legal owner.

Fact: Computer image matching of cartridges fails between 38-62% of the time, depending on whether the cartridges are from the same or different manufacturers.[16]

Fact: "Automated computer matching systems do not provide conclusive results" requiring that "potential candidates be manually reviewed".[17]

Fact: Criminals currently remove serial numbers from stolen guns to hide their origin. The same simple shop tools can change a ballistic profile within minutes. "The minor alteration required less than 5 minutes of labor".[18] Criminals will make changing ballistic profiles part of their standard procedures.

Myth: Ballistic imaging is used in Maryland and New York and solves many crimes

Fact: Not so far. New York has not reported a single prosecution based on matched casings or bullets[19, 20, 21] and Maryland had only a single instance in 2005.[22] The cost for this lack of success in Maryland exceeds $2,500,000 a year, and in New York it exceeds $4,000,000.

Fact: In Syracuse, the police have submitted fewer than 400 handguns for ballistic testing over a three-year span because the system is inefficient.[23]

Myth: A ballistic database is inexpensive to create/maintain

Fact: "... [A] huge inventory [of possible matches] will be generated for manual review." "[The] number of candidate cases will be so large as to be impractical and will likely create logistic complications so great that they cannot be effectively addressed".[24]

Myth: Police want a ballistic database

Fact: "The National Fraternal Order of Police does not support any Federal requirement to register privately owned firearms with the Federal government," the group said. "And, even if such a database is limited to firearms manufactured in the future, the cost to create and maintain such a system, with such small chances that it would be used to solve a firearm crime, suggests to the F.O.P. that these are law enforcement dollars best spent elsewhere."[25]

Fact: "We in law enforcement know it will not, does not, cannot work. Then, no one has considered the hundreds of millions of guns in the US that have never been registered or tested or printed."[26]

Fact: "One, the barrel is one of the most easily changed parts of many guns and two, the barrel, and the signature it leaves on a bullet, is constantly changing."[27]

1. *Ballistic Imaging*, Daniel Cork, John Rolph, Eugene Meieran, Carol Petrie, National Research Council, 2008
2. *Feasibility of a Ballistics Imaging Database for All New Handgun Sales*, Frederic Tulleners, California Department of Justice, Bureau of Forensic Services, October 2001 (henceforth *FBID*)
3. *Feasibility of a Ballistics Imaging Database for All New Handgun Sales*, Frederic Tulleners, California Department of Justice, Bureau of Forensic Services, October 2001 (henceforth *FBID*)
4. *Feasibility of a Ballistics Imaging Database for All New Handgun Sales*, Frederic Tulleners, California Department of Justice, Bureau of Forensic Services, October 2001 (henceforth *FBID*)
5. *Feasibility of a Ballistics Imaging Database for All New Handgun Sales*, Frederic Tulleners, California Department of Justice, Bureau of Forensic Services, October 2001 (henceforth *FBID*)
6. *Handbook of Firearms & Ballistics: Examining and Interpreting Forensic Evidence*, Heard, 1997.
7. *Ballistic Imaging*, Daniel Cork, John Rolph, Eugene Meieran, Carol Petrie, National Research Council, 2008
8. *Ballistics 'fingerprinting' not foolproof*, Baltimore Sun, October 15, 2002
9. *AFTE Journal*, George G. Krivosta, Winter 2006 edition, Suffolk County Crime Laboratory, Hauppauge, New York
10. *Ballistic Imaging*, Daniel Cork, John Rolph, Eugene Meieran, Carol Petrie, National Research Council, 2008
11. *Maryland State Police Report Recommends Suspending Ballistics ID System*, Col. Thomas E. Hutchins, the state police superintendent, WBAL-TV web site, January 17, 2005
12. *Maryland State Police Report Recommends Suspending Ballistics ID*

System, Col. Thomas E. Hutchins, the state police superintendent, WBAL-TV web site, January 17, 2005, Sgt. Thornnie Rouse, Maryland State police spokesman

13. *MD-IBIS Progress Report #2*, Maryland State Police Forensic Sciences Division, September 2004

14. *Protecting America*, Bureau of Alcohol, Tobacco and Firearms, 1992

15. *Armed and Considered Dangerous*, U.S. Department of Justice, 1986

16. *Feasibility of a Ballistics Imaging Database for All New Handgun Sales*, Frederic Tulleners, California Department of Justice, Bureau of Forensic Services, October 2001

17. *Feasibility of a Ballistics Imaging Database for All New Handgun Sales*, Frederic Tulleners, California Department of Justice, Bureau of Forensic Services, October 2001

18. *Feasibility of a Ballistics Imaging Database for All New Handgun Sales*, Frederic Tulleners, California Department of Justice, Bureau of Forensic Services, October 2001

19. *NY ballistic database firing blanks?* Associated Press, June 3, 2004

20. *Ballistics 'fingerprinting' not foolproof*, Baltimore Sun, October 15, 2002

21. *Townsend backs New Rule on Sale of Assault Rifles*, Washington Post, October 30, 2002

22. *Ballistics Database Yields 1st Conviction*, Washington Post, April 2, 2005

23. *400 guns wait to be traced by Syracuse police*, The Post-Standard, December 8, 2002.

24. *Ballistics 'fingerprinting' not foolproof*, Baltimore Sun, October 15, 2002

25. *F.O.P. Viewpoint: Ballistics Imaging and Comparison Technology*, FOP Grand Lodge, October 2002

26. Joe Horn, Detective, Retired, Los Angeles County Sheriff's Dept., Small Arms Expert

27. Ted Deeds, chief operating officer of The Law Enforcement Alliance of America, Dodge Globe, Oct 24, 2002

Miscellaneous Gun Control Information

Firearms in the United States

Nobody is sure of exactly how many firearms are in circulation. This stems from a long history of no regulations on firearm ownership. In Gun Facts, we rely on the estimates presented in *Targeting Guns*, which used estimates from before the creation of the federal Bureau of Alcohol, Tobacco and Firearms (BATF) augmented with their annual Firearms Commerce Reports.

We have continued that approach in our own estimates.

Number of firearms in America: Between 223,000,000[1] and 290,000,000[2]

Handguns in circulation: 122,006,701 (2010)

Households with Firearms: Between 40-50%.

The number of households with firearms is impossible to accurately measure due to survey responses. Long ago criminologists noticed that women reporting a firearm in the home was much lower than men. This could mean any number of things, some being:

- Some women might not know there is a firearm in their house.
- Women don't like admitting guns are in their homes.
- Men lie in false bravado.

With the number of women admitting to firearm ownership rising, the first is considered most likely. This means that previous under reporting raises the percentages. Another problem is that some people do not like disclosing they own firearms. One survey, which concluded household firearm ownership was around 30% was conducted by the government. One explanation was that some people did not want their ownership recorded such that the government could take action (e.g. confiscation). If this is true for non-government surveys as well, the percentages rise even higher.

Concealed Carry in the United States

As of the summer of 2016:[3]

- 16.3 million concealed carry licensees (this does not include citizen who carry in 11 states that do not require permits).

- Per a Pew poll, 26% of these people carry all the time, which means at any given moment over 4,000,000 citizens are carrying firearms in public.

- The number of women with permits has increased at twice the pace as men with permits.

2,500,500 or 235,700 defensive gun uses (DGU)?

You may have heard that firearms are used 2.5 million times a year for self-defense, and you may also have heard they are only used 235,700 times. The reason is that there are different sources of the data and different ways of measuring.

The 2.5M times number come from criminologist Gary Kleck and his book *Targeting Gun*. Kleck gathered many surveys from both criminologists and media sources, and the midpoint was 2.5M DGUs a year (one of the surveys he reported was significantly higher and another one was lower, but most were in the 2-2.5M range).

The 235,700 number comes from the National Crime Victimization Survey (NCVS). One important methodological difference in the NCVS is that it entails personal, face-to-face engagements with government employees (per their methodology documentation "all interviews are done by telephone whenever possible, except for the first interview, which is primarily conducted in person"). There is also the potential for self-incrimination that may prevent reporting of some DGUs to this government survey. A victim may have a strong reluctance to talk to a government agent about a firearm brandishing incident (which are 98% of DGUs) because they may not know the act was 100% legal. Thus, to assure they are not victimized by the legal system, they avoid reporting DGUs to this government survey. Another criticism of the NCVS is that questions concerning gun-use are never asked unless the interviewee first indicates that they were "a victim of a crime." Since some people who successfully avoid being a victim by using a gun reply that they have not been victimized, they are never asked the question about use of a firearm.

Because of this, some criminologists believe there is a self-reporting bias in the NCVS (e.g., people don't like to tell the government they own or used a gun). Thus, this low number from the NCVS is considered to be an outlier and not reliable compared to other, broader and more standardized measures.

British Crime Statistics

The U.K. measures crime using two different processes:

British Crime Survey (BCS): The Home Office conducts surveys of the population to determine how often subjects have been affected by criminal activity. Data is projected to reflect the entire population.

Police reporting: Crimes are reported to the police and nationwide, census-level statistics are summarized.

The BCS has been reporting a declining crime rate in the UK while police reporting has shown an increase. The BCS has routinely been criticized because it under reports crime due to the following factors:

- Murdered and imprisoned people do not answer surveys
- Some crimes are not surveyed when victims are below age 16[4]
- Crime against institutions (bank robbery, etc.) are not included

The crime reporting system isn't without flaws either. Crimes are recorded at final disposition (conviction/acquittal), leaving many crimes completely unreported.[5]
These deficiencies are so significant that even the British government does not believe the accuracy of the BCS.

"[T]he BCS did not record 'various categories of violent crime', including murder and rape, retail crime, drug-taking, or offences in which the victims were aged below 16. The most reliable measure of crime is that which is reported to the police. We're facing over a million violent crimes a year for the first time in history."[6]

Screen shot of Gun Violence Archive misdefinition

- Age: 24
- Age Group: Adult 18+
- Gender: Male
- Status: Unharmed, Arrested

Incident Characteristics

- Non-Shooting Incident
- Drug Involvement
- Possession (Gun(s) found during comission of other crimes)

Notes

2 Firearms seized during narcotics investigation

Gun control groups tend to cite the BCS reports because it supports their narrative that Britain's gun control laws lower crime. Criminologists tend to use the police reporting system because it more closely matches the FBI Uniform Crime Statistics used in the United States.

More curious are the sudden leaps in reported violent crime when the British Home Office enforced standardized methods for recording reported crime (which led the Home Office to claim crime reports to be of poor quality, and thus rely on the suspect survey mechanism): The 1998 changes to the Home Office Counting Rules had a very significant impact on violent crime; the numbers of such crimes recorded by the police increased by 83 per cent as a result of the 1998 changes ... The National Crime Recording Standard (NCRS), introduced in April 2002, again resulted in increased recording of violent crimes particularly for less serious violent offenses.[7]

Gun Violence Archive

There are numerous critiques of the Gun Violence Archives, which combined indicate that this is a non-viable criminology resource. The primary problem is a lack of reach. Whereas the FBI Uniform Crime Reporting system spans the country, the Gun Violence Archive "... numbers are found through 2,000 LEO, government and media sources." There are nearly 18,000 law enforcement agencies in the United States. If we were generous and assumed that most of the outlets from which the Gun Violence Archives find incident reports were law enforcement, they are still examining only 11% of the agencies. Since media reports make up a significant amount of the Gun Violence Archive's reporting, odds are the reach into official agencies, which have uniform tracking methodologies, is much lower than 11%. Another problem is the definition of "gun violence" employed by the Gun Violence Archive is often misused. Their definition is "... all incidents of death or injury or threat with firearms." This leads to episodes like the one shown here, clipped from the Gun Violence Archive web site, being included in their tallies along with homicides and woundings. Notice that this was a "non-shooting" incident. The takeaway is that the Gun Violence Archive is a non-serious tool for understanding crime, violence and how guns fit into the situation.

Confused terms in gun control policy

Assault rifle and assault weapon:

Assault *rifles* are real, and are a specific type of military weapon classified by the Department of Defense. These are not generally available to the public. Assault *weapon* is a legislative term, and means whatever the law says. In a paper promoting the extension of the federal assault weapons ban, the Law Center to Prevent Gun Violence admitted that various "assault weapons" laws across the nation covered anywhere from 19 to 75 banned firearms, six differing generic classification schemes and several legal systems for banning more firearms without specific legislative action.

Negligent discharge and accidental shooting

Negligent discharges are defined as "a discharge of a firearm involving culpable carelessness." In other words, a person did not have their firearm properly secured or handled it in a careless fashion. Accidental shootings include negligent discharges, but include other activities such as unintended targets, people walking into a line of fire, down-range hunting accidents and more.

Genocide and Gun Control[8]

Outside of war, the greatest loss of human life in the 20th century came from governments. In nearly every case, disarmament preceded mass murder. Though some nations have been functionally disarmed without such atrocities, it is worth remembering:

- In 1911, Turkey established gun control. Subsequently, from 1915 to 1917, 1.5-million Armenians, deprived of the means to defend themselves, were rounded up and killed.

- In 1929, the Soviet Union established gun control. Then, from 1929 to 1953, approximately 20-millon dissidents were rounded up and killed.

- In 1938 Germany established gun control. From 1939 to 1945 over 13-million Jews, gypsies, homosexuals, mentally ill, union leaders, Catholics and others, unable to fire a shot in protest, were rounded up and killed.

- In 1935, China established gun control. Subsequently, between 1948 and 1952, over 20-million dissidents were rounded up and killed.

- In 1956, Cambodia enshrined gun control. In just two years (1975-1977) over one million "educated" people were rounded up and killed.

- In 1964, Guatemala locked in gun control. From 1964 to 1981, over 100,000 Mayan Indians were rounded up and killed as a result of their inability to defend themselves.

- In 1970, Uganda embraced gun control. Over the next nine years over 300,000 Christians were rounded up and killed.

Over 56-million people have died because of gun control in the last century

1. *Guns Used in Crime*, Bureau of Justice Statistics, Marianne W. Zawitz, 1995

2. *Small Arms Survey*, Graduate Institute of International Studies, 2008

3. *Concealed Carry Permit Holders Across the United States*: 2016, Lott, Crime Prevention Research Center, July 2016

4. This is a serious omission as most gang crime is committed by and against young people.

5. *Fear in Britain,* Dr. Paul Gallant and Dr. Joanne Eisen, National Review, July 18, 2000

6. *Row over figures as crime drops 5%*, David Davis, Shadow Home Secretary, The Guardian, July 22, 2004

7. *Crime in England and Wales 2005/06,* British Home Office, July 2006

8. *Death by Gun Control: The Human Cost of Victim Disarmament,*" Aaron Zelman & Richard W. Stevens, 2001

Microstamping

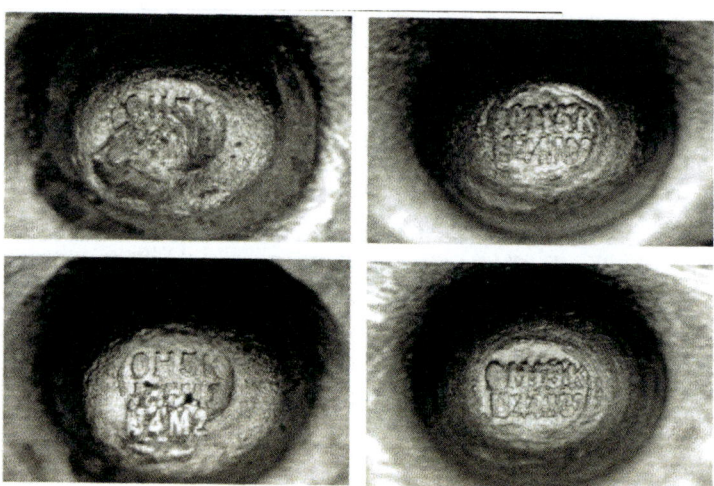

Background: Microstamping is a proposed means for imprinting unique serial numbers onto cartridges fired from a gun. Similar to "ballistic fingerprinting," it allegedly helps police identify what firearm might have been used in a crime. Microstamping uses precision equipment to remove microscopic amounts of metal from the tip of the firing pin

Myth: Independent testing by forensic technologists shows the technology is reliable

Fact: Firing pins are readily removable and swappable in most models of handguns with inexpensive replacement parts. Criminals who file down serial numbers on the sides of guns won't hesitate to file or exchange firing pins.

Fact: 46% of impressions ranked as "unsatisfactory" (i.e., illegible) after only ten rounds.[1]

Fact: Reloaded ammo (which is extremely common due to the economics of recycling casings and home reloading tools) will make prosecuting cases nearly impossible once the "reloaded ammo" defense is raised (for microstamping that imprints case sides). A *case* may have two or more markings, making the final shooter impossible to identify.

Myth: Filing the firing pin will make the gun inoperable

Fact: Firing pins are designed to be pushed deeply into the primer (igniter) of the round. The depth of the engraving (approximately 0.005 inch)[2] is vastly smaller than the tolerance of the firing pin's drive depth.

Fact: In a test, the engravings were removed using a 50-year-old knife sharpening stone in less than a minute. The firearm still operated correctly after the filing.[3]

Myth: The cost per firearm will be cheap

Fact: The National Shooting Sports Foundation, the representative for firearm manufacturers, estimates the cost will be upwards of $150 per firearm, more than tripling the price of self-protection and making it unaffordable for low-income people.[4] The Brady Campaign dispute those with firearm manufacturing experience claiming micro-stamping would cost only 50¢?

Myth: The numbers will let police find the gun's owner and help solve crimes

Fact: Since many crime guns are stolen property,[5] finding the original owner does not help solve the crime.

1. *NanoTag™ Markings From Another Perspective*, George G. Krivosta, Suffolk County Crime Laboratory, Hauppauge, New York, Winter 2006 edition of the AFTE Journal

2. *NanoTagTM Markings From Another Perspective*, George G. Krivosta, Suffolk County Crime Laboratory, Hauppauge, New York, Winter 2006 edition of the AFTE Journal

3. *NanoTagTM Markings From Another Perspective*, George G. Krivosta, Suffolk County Crime Laboratory, Hauppauge, New York, Winter 2006 edition of the AFTE Journal

4. *Etched bullets interest law enforcement*, The Record, September 25, 2006

5. *Armed and Considered Dangerous*, U.S. Department of Justice, 1986

Assorted Myths

Myth: 30,000 people are killed with guns every year.

Fact: 61% of these deaths are suicides[1] (80% in Canada[2]). Numerous studies have shown that the presence or absence of a firearm does not change the overall (i.e., gun plus non-gun) suicide rate. This 30,000 number also includes justifiable homicides (self-defense) and accidents.

Myth: Gun ownership is falling in the United States

Fact: Two surveys (ABC/POST and Gallup) show household ownership rates have remained steady, while two others (Pew and GSS) show ownership dropping.

Poll	Gun Ownership Trend	Registered Voter Isolation
ABC/Post	Steady	Yes
Gallup	Steady	Yes
Pew	Declining	No
GSS	Declining	No

The former report on registered voters, who have to be citizens to vote in federal elections. The latter polls everyone regardless of citizenship status. With the non-citizen population growing 37% in less than 30 years, and now claiming about 11% of the total population, this is a key differentiator.

Myth: 1,000 people die each day from guns

Fact: 25% of this unreliable figure[3] includes "direct war deaths," and another 14% are suicides. The bulk of the rest come from violence-prone and near-lawless localities.

Fact: The source for this raw data admits, "A complete dataset on people killed in conflict—directly or indirectly—does not exist. All published figures are estimates based on incomplete information."[4]

Fact: Indeed, the definition of "gun" seems to be very broad: "… revolvers and self-loading pistols, rifles and carbines, assault rifles, sub-machine guns, and light machine guns." Light weapons are "… heavy machine guns, hand-held under-barrel and mounted grenade launchers, portable antitank and anti-aircraft guns, recoilless rifles, portable launchers of anti-tank and antiaircraft missile systems, and mortars of less than 100mm caliber." And they admit to the problem of a broad definition: "The Survey uses the terms 'small arms,' 'firearms,' and 'weapons,' interchangeably. Unless the context dictates otherwise, no distinction is intended between commercial firearms (e.g. hunting rifles), and small arms and "light" weapons designed for military use (e.g. assault rifles)."[5]

Myth: The Brady Campaign has a good ranking system of state gun control laws.

Fact: There is zero correlation between the letter grades given by the Brady Campaign and the violent crime or murder rate in those states, making the Brady grade irrelevant (see chart at right).[6]

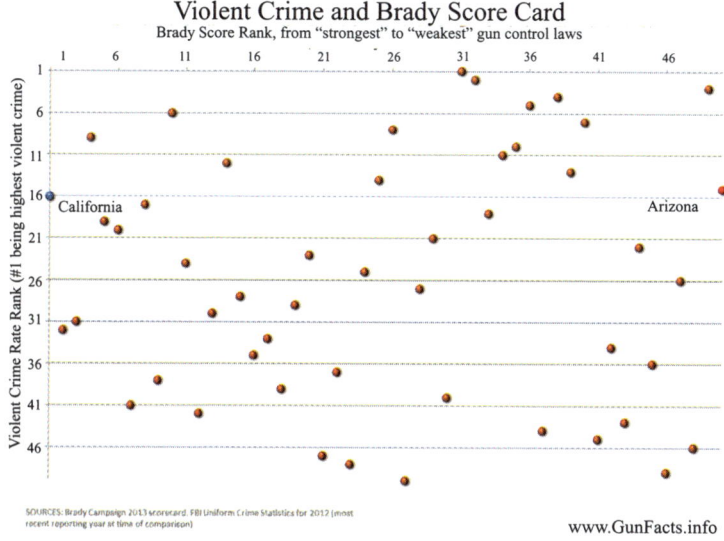

Violent Crime and Brady Score Card
Brady Score Rank, from "strongest" to "weakest" gun control laws

SOURCES: Brady Campaign 2013 scorecard. FBI Uniform Crime Statistics for 2012 (most recent reporting year at time of comparison)

www.GunFacts.info

Fact: The states that the Brady campaign rank first and last have nearly identical violent crime rates.

Myth: High-capacity magazines lead to more deadly shootings

Fact: Much of this myth comes from the fact that the general availability of high-capacity handguns briefly preceded the rise in the crack cocaine trade, which brought a new kind of violence in local drugs wars.[7]

Fact: The number of shots fired by criminals has not changed significantly even with the increased capacity of handguns and other firearms. Indeed, the number of shots from revolvers (all within 6-8 round capacity) and semi-automatics were about the same – 2.04 vs. 2.53.[8] In a crime or gun battle, there is seldom time or need to shoot more.

Fact: The average magazine swap time for a non-expert shooter is 2-3 seconds. In the case of the Newtown Sandy Hook massacre, the murderer performed 10 magazine changes, or about 30 of the ~600 seconds that lapsed from him entering the building to when the police arrived. A 10-round restriction would have raised it to only 46 seconds and thus would have saved nobody.

Fact: Firearm homicides declined from 6.3 to 4.2 (per 100,000 population) from 1981 through 1998, when the increase in semi-automatics and large capacity handguns were rising at a fast rate.[9] Fatal shootings of police officers declined sharply from 1988 through 1993.[10]

Fact: Drug dealers tend to be "more deliberate in their efforts to kill their victims by shooting them multiple times."[11]

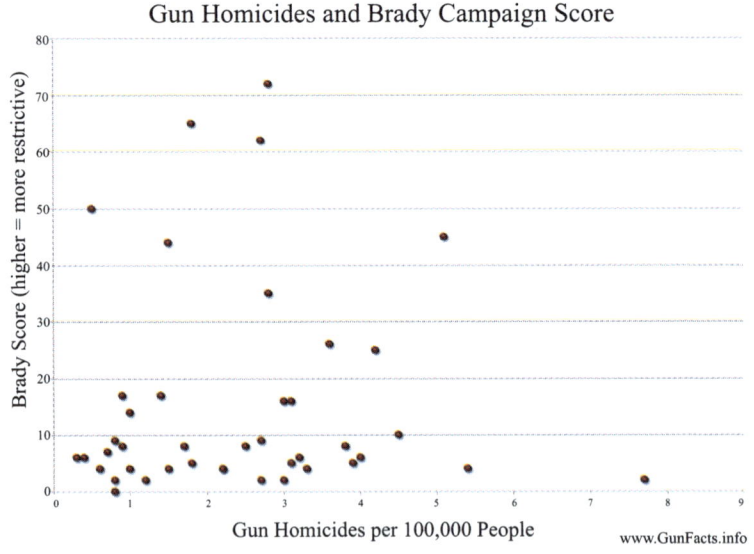

Gun Homicides and Brady Campaign Score

www.GunFacts.info

Myth: "Universal" background checks will reduce crime

Fact: With nearly 40% of crime guns coming from black-market street dealers peddling stolen and recycled guns, and another 40% coming from "acquaintance" purchases[12] (friends, other criminals, illegal straw sales) expanded background checks won't stop these already off-the-radar transfers.

Fact: Police don't think so – 80% surveyed reject the notion.[13]

Myth: Homicides went up when Missouri repealed their permit-to-purchase (licensing) law

Fact: The homicide rate in Missouri has actually dropped in that period, according to the FBI's Universal Crime Reporting data.[14]

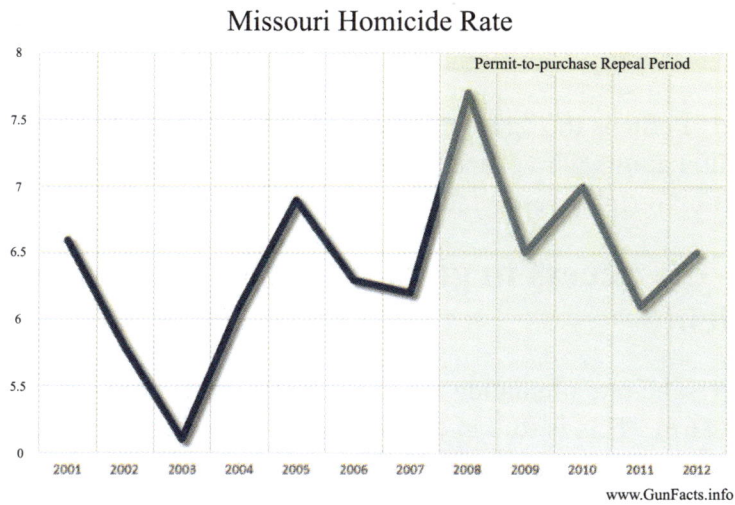

Missouri Homicide Rate

www.GunFacts.info

Myth: Connecticut's permit and background law caused homicide to fall by 40%[15]

Fact: This "study" did not use historical homicide data. Instead it created a statistical model of a "synthetic

Connecticut" that was comprised using 72% of Rhode Island›s data. It is also worth noting that Connecticut›s homicide rate was already in free-fall before the law was passed, dropping 27% from its high in 1993.

Myth: The "powerful gun industry" stops all gun control legislation

Fact: The firearms industry is composed of "small, marginally profitable companies," with combined revenues of $1.5 billion to $2 billion per year, making it politically ineffective.[16]

Fact: Total political contributions from firearm industry members, PACs and employees was under $4.4 million in the 2002 election cycle, which made the industry the 64th ranked contributor. Compare that to $33 million from the American Federation of State, County & Municipal Employees. [17]

Fact: Perhaps the "gun industry" being referenced is the 100+ million adults who peacefully own firearms and do not want their civil rights restricted.

Myth: Access to guns increases the risk of suicide

Fact: The rate of suicide is not affected by the presence of a firearm. This is true in either a time-series analysis (like the chart at right showing the change in handgun supply in the U.S. over time),[18] or through cross-national analysis. For example, Japan has no private handgun ownership (aside from an extremely limited number of licensed Olympic sport shooters), and yet had a suicide rate more than twice that of the United States in 2002.[19]

Fact: The claim derives mainly from one study[20] which has some serious methodology problems including unbalanced high/low state counts, inclusion of Hawaii (a known outlier) and intermixing mental health and drug use as confounding variables.

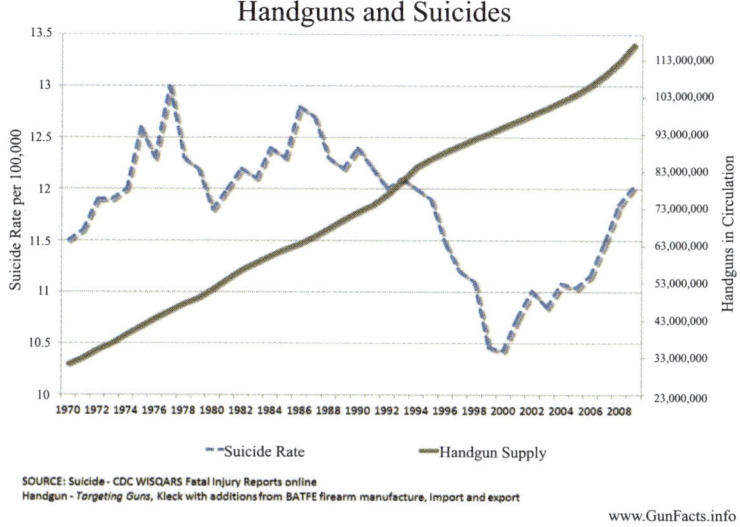

Handguns and Suicides

SOURCE: Suicide - CDC WISQARS Fatal Injury Reports online
Handgun - *Targeting Guns*, Kleck with additions from BATFE firearm manufacture, import and export

www.GunFacts.info

Myth: States with background checks and waiting periods have lower suicide rates

Fact: This study ("Handgun Legislation and Changes in Statewide Overall Suicides Rates") had significant methodology flaws, including being a time-series study covering just one year and omitting a number necessary variables.

Myth: States with The Most Gun Laws See the Fewest Gun-Related Deaths

Fact: This study [21] includes suicides, which account for approximately 2/3rd of "gun deaths". As has been shown before, gun availability does not change the probability of a successful suicide.

Myth: Individuals who commit suicide are more likely to have had access to guns[22]

Fact: This is a classic causal effect. If someone decides to commit suicide, and they choose to use a gun, they will first acquire a gun. As noted before, the total rate of suicide does not change when a gun is present because the victim will choose a different method.

Myth: The only purpose for a gun is to kill people

Fact: Guns are used for self-defense 2,500,000 times a year in the United States.[23]

Fact: Guns are used as a deterrent to crime even when no rounds are fired.[24]

Fact: Guns are used in sports including hunting, target practice, practical pistol, scenario simulation, skeet, etc.

Myth: 89% of mayors want congress to create tougher gun control laws

Fact: This *famously flawed survey* (which the publication admitted was not scientific), cherry picked a full 76% of the respondents from the Michael Bloomberg gun-control group Mayors Against Illegal Guns.

1. Center for Disease Control, WISQARS Fatal Injury Reports
2. *Death Involving Firearms*, Kathryn Wilkins, Health Report vol. 16, no 4, Statistics Canada.
3. *Bringing the global gun crisis under control*, IANSA, 2006 citing Small Arms Survey.
4. Small Arms Survey 2005, www.smallarmssurvey.org.
5. Small Arms Survey 2002, www.smallarmssurvey.org.
6. 2012 Brady Campaign Scorecard, Center for Disease Control firearm

homicides statistics

7. *Targeting Guns*, Gary Kleck, Aldine Transaction, 1997.

8. *Urban firearm deaths: A five-year perspective*, Michael McGonigal, John Cole, William Schwab, Donald Kauder, Michael Rotondo, Peter Angood, Journal of Trauma, 1993.

9. Center for Disease Control WISQARS.

10. *Firearm injury from crime*, Marianne Zawitz, 1996, Bureau of Justice Statistics.

11. *Epidemiological changes in gunshot wounds in Washington D.C*, Webster, Champion, Gainer and Sykes, Archives of Surgery, 1992.

12. *Firearm Use by Offenders*, Bureau of Justice Statistics, February 2002.

13. *Gun Policy & Law Enforcement*, PoliceOne, March 2013

14. FBI, Uniform Crime Reports, online database

15. *Association between Connecticut's permit-to-purchase handgun law and homicides*, Webster, Stuart, Vernick, Rudolph, Johns Hopkins Center for Gun Policy and Research, 2015

16. New York Times, Mar. 18, 2000.

17. OpenSecrets.org, May 2003.

18. FBI Uniform Crime Statistics online, BATFE Firearm Commerce Report for 2002.

19. FBI Uniform Crime Statistics, World Health Organization Suicide Prevention country reports (online).

20. *Household Firearm Ownership and Rates of Suicide Across the 50 United States*, Miller, Steven, Lippmann, Azrael, Hemenway, Journal or Trauma, April 2007

21. *The States With The Most Gun Laws See The Fewest Gun-Related Deaths*, Nation Journal, January 2016

22. *Mental Illness, Previous Suicidality, and Access to Guns in the United States*, Ilgen, Zivin, McCammon, Valenstein, 2008 American Psychiatric Association.

23. *Targeting Guns*, Gary Kleck, Aldine Transaction, 1997

24. *Targeting Guns*, Gary Kleck, Aldine Transaction, 1997

Second Amendment

Justification clause: "A well regulated Militia being necessary to the security of a free State,"

Rights clause: "the right of the people to keep and bear Arms shall not be infringed."

The justification clause does not modify, restrict, or deny the rights clause.[1]

Myth: The Supreme Court ruled the Second Amendment is not an individual right

Fact: In *D.C. v Heller* the Supreme Court (2008) firmly established the 2nd Amendment is an individual right, as they had in Cruikshank and Dred Scott.

Fact: In *McDonald v Chicago* (2010) the Supreme Court concluded the right is incorporated against the states via the 14th Amendment.

Fact: Of 300 decisions of the federal and state courts that have taken a position on the meaning of the Second Amendment or the state analogs to it, only 10 have claimed that the right to keep and bear arms is not an individual right. Many of the other decisions struck down gun control laws because they conflicted with the Second Amendment, such as *State v. Nunn* (Ga. 1846).[2]

Myth: The Second Amendment is a collective right, not an individual right

Fact: St. George Tucker, any early legal commentator and authority on the original meaning of the constitution wrote in Blackstone's Commentaries "… nor will the constitution permit any prohibition of arms to the people" [3]

Fact: The Second Amendment was listed in a Supreme Court ruling as an individual right.[4]

Fact: The Supreme Court specifically reaffirmed that the right to keep and bear arms did not belong to the government.[5]

Fact: In 22 of the 27 instances where the Supreme Court mentions the Second Amendment, they quote the rights clause and not the justification clause.

Fact: Courts disagree. "We find that the history of the Second Amendment reinforces the plain meaning of its text, namely that it protects individual Americans in their right to keep and bear arms whether or not they are a member of a select militia or performing active military service or training" and "We reject the collective rights and sophisticated collective rights models for interpreting the Second Amendment" [6]

Fact: Citizens disagree. 62% believe the 2nd Amendment guarantees an individual right, while a mere 28% believe it protects the power of the states to form militias.[7]

Fact: There are 23 state constitutions with RKBA clauses adopted between the Revolution and 1845, and 20 of them are explicitly individual in nature, only three have "for the common defense…." or other "collective rights" clauses.[8]

Fact: James Madison, considered to be the author of the Bill of Rights, wrote that the Bill of Rights was "calculated to secure the personal rights of the people". He never excluded the Second Amendment from this statement.

Fact: Patrick Henry commented on the Swiss militia model (still in use today) noting that they maintain their independence without "a mighty and splendid President" or a standing army.[9]

Fact: "The congress of the United States possesses no power to regulate, or interfere with the domestic concerns, or police of any state: it belongs not to them to establish any rules respecting the rights of property; nor will the constitution permit any prohibition of arms to the people; or of peaceable assemblies by them, for any purposes whatsoever, and in any number, whenever they may see occasion."[10]

Fact: Tench Coxe, in Remarks on the First Part of the Amendments to the Federal Constitution said: "As civil rulers, not having their duty to the people duly before them, may attempt to tyrannize, and as the military forces which must be occasionally raised to defend our country, might pervert their power to the injury of their fellow-citizens, the people are confirmed by the next article in their right to keep and bear their private arms."

Myth: The Heller Decision created new law

Fact: In the Dred Scott case of 1856, the Supreme Court listed the protected rights of citizens and explicitly listed the right to keep and bear arms, and gave this right equal weight to the other freedoms enumerated in the constitution.

Fact: In *United States v. Cruikshank*, 92 U.S. 542 (1876), the Supreme Court ruled:

- An individual right to arms predated the constitution.
- The Second Amendment was a prohibition against Congress from disarming citizens.

Myth: The Second Amendment was established to control slaves

Fact: The basis of the Second Amendment arose from the British disarming Americans in the time leading up to the revolution. The first state to declare a civilian right to arms (1776) was Pennsylvania, a non-slave state. Vermont (1777) and Massachusetts (1780) did so as well, and all this occurred before the Second Amendment was drafted. When slaves were emancipated, the Freedmen Bureau Act provided emancipated slaves "the constitutional right to bear arms."

Myth: The "militia" clause is to arm the National Guard

Fact: "Militia is a Latin abstract noun, meaning "military service", not an "armed group", and that is the way the Latin-literate Founders used it. To the Romans, "military service" included law enforcement and disaster response. Today "militia" might be more meaningfully translated as "defense service", associated with a "defense duty", which attaches to individuals as much as to groups of them, organized or otherwise. When we are alone, we are all militias of one. In the broadest sense, militia is the exercise of civic virtue.[11]

Fact: The Dick Act of 1903 designated the National Guard as the **"organized militia"** and that all other citizens were the **"unorganized militia"** – thus the National Guard is only part of the militia, and the whole militia is composed of the population at large. Before 1903, the National Guard had no federal definition as part of the militia at all.

Fact: The first half of the Second Amendment is called the "justification clause". Justification clauses appear in many state constitutions, and cover liberties including right to trial, freedom of the press, free speech, and more. ***Denying gun rights based on the justification clause means we would have to deny free speech rights on the same basis.***[12]

Fact: The origin of the phrase "a well regulated militia" comes from a 1698 treatise "A Discourse of Government with Relation to Militias" by Andrew Fletcher, in which the term "well regulated" was equated with "well-behaved" or "disciplined".[13]

Fact: "We have found no historical evidence that the Second Amendment was intended to convey militia power to the states, limit the federal government›s power to maintain a standing army, or applies only to members of a select militia while on active duty. All of the evidence indicates that the Second Amendment, like other parts of the Bill of Rights, applies to and protects individual Americans."[14]

Fact: "The plain meaning of the right of the people to keep arms is that it is an individual, rather than a collective, right and is not limited to keeping arms while engaged in active military service or as a member of a select militia such as the National Guard ..."[15]

Fact: Most of the 13 original states (and many colonies/ territories that became states after ratification of the Constitution and before or shortly after ratification of the Bill of Rights) had their own constitutions, and it is from these that the original Bill of Rights was distilled. The state constitutions of that time had many "right to keep and bear arms" clauses that clearly guaranteed an individual right. Some examples include:

> Connecticut: Every citizen has a right to bear arms in defense of himself and the state.
>
> Kentucky: ... the right of the citizens to bear arms in defense of themselves and the State shall not be questioned.
>
> Pennsylvania: That the people have a right to bear arms for the defense of themselves and the state; ... The right of the citizens to bear arms in defense of themselves and the State shall not be questioned.
>
> Rhode Island: The right of the people to keep and bear arms shall not be infringed.
>
> Vermont: ... the people have a right to bear arms for the defense of themselves and the State.

Myth: The Second Amendment allows Congress to regulate ownership of guns for militia purposes

Fact: The phrase "well regulated" was common in the constitutional era, and described things that were in proper order or function. It was not a writ of authority. Borrowing from the Oxford English Dictionary, these examples, both before and after composition of the Second Amendment, show the usage:

> 1709: "If a liberal Education has formed in us well-regulated Appetites and worthy Inclinations."

> 1714: "The practice of all well-regulated courts of justice in the world."

> 1812: "The equation of time ... is the adjustment of the difference of time as shown by a well-regulated clock and a true sun dial."

> 1848: "A remissness for which I am sure every well-regulated person will blame the Mayor."

> 1862: "It appeared to her well-regulated mind, like a clandestine proceeding."

> 1894: "The newspaper, a never wanting adjunct to every well-regulated American embryo city."

Myth: U.S. v. Cruikshank denied an individual right to bear arms

Fact: The court ruled that both the 2nd Amendment right to bear arms and the 1st Amendment right to assembly were "preexisting rights", and that it was incumbent upon the states to enforce that right. Specifically, the court ruled:

> *The right was not created by the amendment; neither was its continuance guaranteed, except*

as against congressional interference. For their protection in its enjoyment, therefore, the people must look to the States. ...

Myth: U.S. v. Miller said that the Second Amendment is not an individual right

Fact: The Miller case specifically held that specific types of guns might be protected by the Second Amendment. It depended on whether a gun had militia use, and the court wanted evidence presented confirming that citizens have a right to military style weapons.

Since no evidence was taken at the trial level in lower courts, they remanded the case for a new trial. Specifically, the court said:

> "The signification attributed to the term Militia appears from the debates in the Convention, the history and legislation of Colonies and States, and the writings of approved commentators. *These show plainly enough that the Militia comprised all males physically capable of acting in concert for the common defense.* "A body of citizens enrolled for military discipline." And further, that ordinarily when called for service *these men were expected to appear bearing arms supplied by themselves and of the kind in common use at the time.*" "In the absence of any evidence tending to show that possession or use of a 'shotgun having a barrel of less than 18 inches in length' at this time has some reasonable relationship to the preservation or efficiency of a well-regulated militia, we cannot say that the Second Amendment guarantees the right to keep and

bear such an instrument. Certainly it is not within judicial notice that this weapon is any part of the ordinary military equipment or that its use could contribute to the common defense."

Fact: Even the US government agreed. Here are some sentences from the brief filed by the government in the appeal to the Supreme Court: "The Second Amendment does not grant to the people the right to keep and bear arms, but merely recognizes the prior existence of that right and prohibits its infringement by Congress." "The 'arms' referred to in the Second Amendment are, moreover, those which ordinarily are used for military or public defense purposes ..." "The Second Amendment does not confer upon the people the right to keep and bear arms; it is one of the provisions of the Constitution which, recognizing the prior existence of a certain right, declares that it shall not be infringed by Congress. Thus, the right to keep and bear arms is not a right granted by the Constitution and therefore is not dependent upon that instrument for its source."

Fact: The Federal 8th Circuit Court of Appeals holds that the Miller case protects an individual right to keep and bear arms. "Although an individual›s right to bear arms is constitutionally protected, see *United States v. Miller* ..."[16]

Fact: Federal courts reject the myth. "We conclude that Miller does not support the [government's] collective rights or sophisticated collective rights approach to the Second Amendment."[17] They continue, "There is no evidence in the text of the Second Amendment, or any other part of the Constitution, that the words 'we the people' have a different connotation within the Second Amendment than when employed elsewhere ...".

Summary of various court decisions concerning gun rights

Decisions that explicitly recognized that the Second Amendment guarantees an individual right to purchase, possess or carry firearms, and that it limits the authority of both federal and state governments:

- ***Parker v. D.C.***, Fed (2007) (confirmed an individual right to keep arms and overturned a handgun ban).

- ***U.S. v. Emerson***, 5 Fed (1999) (confirmed an individual right requiring compelling government interest for regulation).

- ***Nunn v. State***, 1 Ga. 243, 250, 251 (1846) (struck down a ban on the sale of small, easily concealed handguns as violating the Second Amendment).

- ***State v. Chandler***, 5 La.An. 489, 490, 491 (1850) (upheld a ban on concealed carry, but acknowledged that open carry was protected by the Second Amendment).

- ***Smith v. State***, 11 La.An. 633, 634 (1856) (upheld a ban on concealed carry, but recognized as protected by the Second Amendment – "arms there spoken of are such as are borne by a people in war, or at least carried openly").

- ***State v. Jumel***, 13 La.An. 399, 400 (1858) (upheld a ban on concealed carry, but acknowledged a Second Amendment right to carry openly).

- ***Cockrum v. State***, 24 Tex. 394, 401, 402 (1859) (upheld an enhanced penalty for manslaughter with a Bowie knife, but acknowledged that the Second Amendment guaranteed an individual right to possess arms for collective overthrow of the government).

- In Re Brickey, 8 Ida. 597, 70 Pac. 609, 101 Am.St.Rep. 215, 216 (1902) (struck down a ban on open carry of a revolver in Lewiston, Idaho, as violating both Second

Amendment and Idaho Constitution guarantees).

- ***State v. Hart***, 66 Ida. 217, 157 P.2d 72 (1945) (upheld a ban on concealed carry as long as open carry was allowed based on both Second Amendment and Idaho Constitution guarantees).

- ***State v. Nickerson***, 126 Mont. 157, 166 (1952) (striking down a conviction for assault with a deadly weapon, acknowledging a right to carry based on Second Amendment and Montana Constitution guarantees).

- ***U.S. v. Hutzell***, 8 Iowa, 99-3719, (2000) (cite in dictum that "an individual's right to keep and bear arms is constitutionally protected, see United States v. Miller, 307 U.S. 174, 178-79 (1939).

1. Eugene Volokh, Prof. Law, UCLA
2. *For the Defense of Themselves and the State: The Original Intent and Judicial Interpretation of the Right to Keep and Bear Arms*, Clayton Cramer, Praeger Press, 1994
3. *Blackstone's Commentaries,* St. George Tucker, Vol 1. Note D. Part 6. Restraints on Powers of Congress (1803)
4. *Dred Scott, Casey v. Planned Parenthood, U.S. v. Cruikshank* and others
5. *United States v. Miller*
6. *U.S. v. Emerson*, 5th court of Appeals decision, November 2, 2001, No. 99-10331
7. Associated Television News Survey, August 1999, 1,007 likely voters
8. *For the Defense of Themselves and the State: The Original Intent and Judicial Interpretation of the Right to Keep and Bear Arms,* Clayton Cramer, Praeger Press, 1994, cited as an authority in USA v. Emerson (N.D. Texas 1999)
9. *Where Kids and Guns Do Mix*, Stephen P. Halbrook, Wall Street Journal, June 2000
10. *Blackstone's Commentaries,* St. George Tucker, Volume 1, Appendix Note D., 1803 – Tucker's comments provide a number of insights into the consensus for interpretation of the Constitution that prevailed shortly after its ratification, after the debates had settled down and the Constitution was put into practice.
11. *Militia*, The Constitution Society
12. Eugene Volokh, Prof. Law, UCLA, http://www2.law.ucla.edu/volokh/beararms/testimon.htm

13. This document was widely published during the colonial and revolutionary periods, and was the basis for state and federal 'bills of rights'

14. *U.S. v. Emerson*, 5th court of Appeals decision, November 2, 2001, No. 99-10331

15. *U.S. v. Emerson*, 5th court of Appeals decision, November 2, 2001, No. 99-10331

16. *U.S. v. Hutzel*, 8 Iowa, No. 99-3719

17. *U.S. v. Emerson*, 5th court of Appeals decision, November 2, 2001, No. 99-10331

Public Opinion

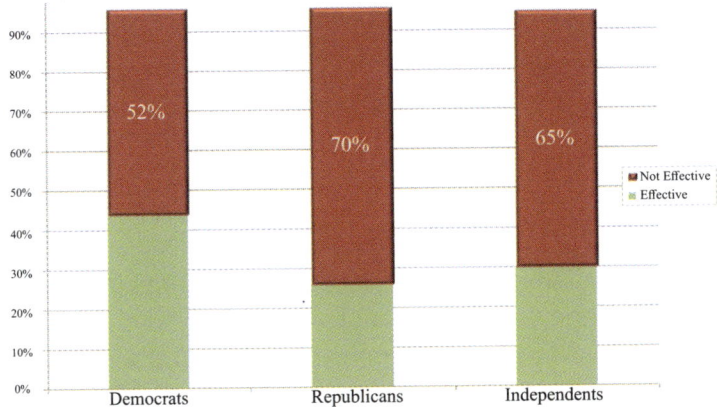

Do you think tighter restrictions on buying and owning guns would be effective or would not be effective in preventing criminals from obtaining guns?

Reason-Rupe Poll, December 4-8, 2013

www.GunFacts.info

Myth: Gun owners are a tiny minority

Fact: The Federal government once estimated that there were well over 65 million gun owners in the U.S. and more than 50% were handgun owners.[1] This number is generally considered low due to the reluctance of many to admit to a government agency that they own a gun. Other estimates indicate that between 41% and 49% of U.S. households are gun-owning households.

Fact: 43% of Americans claim that they own a gun.[2]

Myth: People do not believe that the Second Amendment is an individual right

Fact: A Gallup survey confirms that 73% of Americans believe the 2nd Amendment "guarantees" the right to keep guns, and that a mere 20% believe it exists to enable state militias.[3]

Fact: Surveys show that "52% say it is more important to protect the right of Americans to own guns, while 46% say it is more important to control gun ownership."[4] The split was 29% to 66% in 1999, showing that approval of Second Amendment protections is growing.

Fact: A Zogby poll[5] conducted after the big gun control initiatives of the year 2000 concluded that 75% of Americans believe the right to keep and bear arms is an individual right. In the same year ABC determined the rate to be 77%.[6]

Myth: Most Americans favor gun control

Fact: A CNN/ORC poll has 52% opposing more gun control, and a mere 46% who support it.[7] This agrees with a 2006 Rasmussen survey that found 52% of Americans did not believe more gun control is needed.[8]

Fact: A 2014 Gallup Poll showed that fewer than half of Americans favored stricter gun control, which extended a long-term trend. Barely more than a quarter favor banning handguns (rendered a moot point by the 2008 *Heller* Supreme Court decision).[9]

Fact: Americans believe that parents and popular culture are more responsible for violence in America than firearms.

Cause of Gun Violence	%
The way parents raise their children	45%
Popular culture	26%
Availability of guns	21%
Other	6%
No opinion	2%

Fact: A 1999 survey by the Associated Press showed:

- A plurality (49%) felt enforcing existing laws was the key to reducing violent crime.

- 52% felt that background checks did not help reduce the number of crimes committed with guns.

Fact: A 2000 Zogby telephone survey of 1,201 adults concluded that, by almost a two-to-one margin, Americans prefer enforcement of existing laws instead of new and tougher gun legislation to fight crime. The same poll found that 68% of the public disagrees with cities suing gun makers for the criminal misuse of guns.

Fact: A December 2000 Zogby poll of 1,028 American adults showed that they felt enforcing current laws was the "best way to solve gun violence in America."

	Yes	No
Should the U.S. have stricter gun control laws?	6.73%	92.25%
Do you believe that allowing people to carry concealed weapons reduce crime?	92.22%	7.76%
Do you believe that U.S. cities should sue gun manufacturers to recoup money spent dealing with gun-related crime?	1.96%	98.01%
How would you rate the effectiveness of the Brady Bill and the "assault weapons" ban in preventing the illegal use and distribution of guns?	0.52%	Very effective
	3.79%	Somewhat effective
	6.19%	Somewhat ineffective
	87.27%	Not at all effective
	2.23%	Don't know
Time Magazine, survey of 33,202 adult Americans, 1998		

Fact: A January 2001 Zogby, American Values poll found that 66% of voters felt that the U.S. should spend more money enforcing current laws including mandatory jail time for those who commit a crime with a handgun, while only 26% felt there should be more gun control laws including mandatory gun locks.

Fact: Only 39% believe stricter gun control is needed, down from 43% in an earlier poll.[10]

Fact: An Associated Press poll in April 2000 showed 42% thought stricter enforcement was more likely to cut gun violence. Only 33% said enacting tougher gun laws was better.

Fact: A survey in April 2000 by ABC News/Washington Post asked whether "passing stricter gun control laws" or "stricter enforcement of existing laws" is the best way to curb gun violence. Enforcement was preferred by 53% to 33%.

Fact: 58% percent of Americans believe better enforcement of existing laws "is a better way to reduce handgun violence" than new gun control laws.[11]

How can gun violence be effectively prevented?	People	Percent
Stricter gun control laws	10,841	17.8%
Proper enforcement of current gun control laws	13,587	22.4%
Ban on handguns	8,008	13.2%
Stricter punishment for crimes involving guns	21,596	35.6%
Other	5,094	8.4%
Not sure	1,613	2.7%
AOL.com poll, March 2000		

Fact: A 1999 survey by CBS (hardly a pro-gun organization) found these responses:

- Only 14% of Americans believe that gun control can prevent violence with guns.

- 56% of people said enforcement of existing laws is the better way to reduce violent crime than new gun control laws.

- Only 4% said gun control should be a top issue for the government.

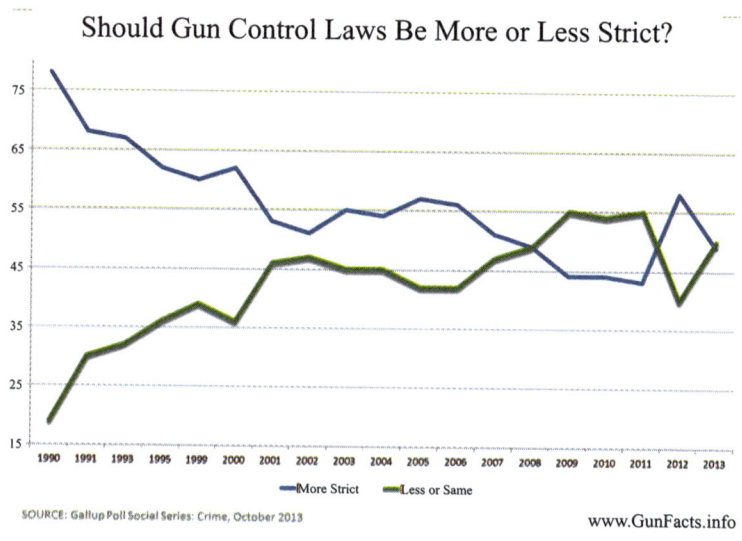

Should Gun Control Laws Be More or Less Strict?

SOURCE: Gallup Poll Social Series: Crime, October 2013

www.GunFacts.info

Myth: More and more Americans support stricter gun control

Fact: The Gallup Poll has been asking Americans this question since 1990 and in the 16 years thereafter, the number supporting stricter gun control has fallen from 78% to 56%.[12]

Fact: Twice as many Americans currently reject the idea of a handgun ban, though a majority favored such a ban in 1959.[13]

Best Way to Reduce Gun Violence	
Enforcing existing laws	52%
Banning handguns	15%
Teach children self-control	15%
Additional congressional legislation	2%
Other	8%
Don't know	2%
Zogby, December 2000	

Myth: People want to ban handguns

Fact: Only 25% of Americans believe handguns should be banned from private ownership and this rate is down from 60% when polling began in the 1950's.[14]

Fact: Even a New York Times poll showed that citizens don't want to ban so-called "assault weapons" by a 50/44 margin[15] though an ABC/Washington Post poll has the split at 53/45.[16] (This is down from an 18/80 split in 1994)

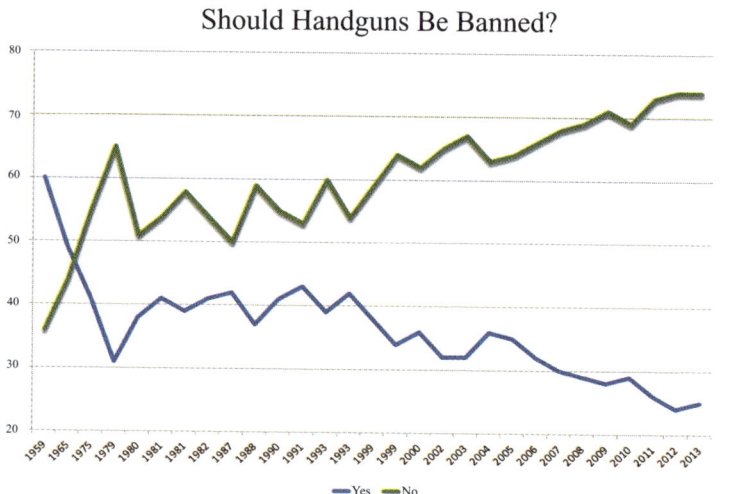

Should Handguns Be Banned?

SOURCE: Gallup Poll Social Series: Crime, October 2013

www.GunFacts.info

Myth: People think gun control stops crime

Fact: Fifty-one percent of Americans think more gun control is more likely to make it harder for law-abiding citizens to purchase a gun rather than keep guns out of the hands of criminals, people with mental illness and suspected terrorists. Only 38% disagree.[17]

Myth: People oppose concealed carry

Fact: 56% say more concealed weapons would make country safer.[18]

Fact: Ignoring for a moment that 42 states have enacted "shall issue" concealed carry laws (and two more never bothered to outlaw concealed carry), a 2009 survey showed 83% support concealed carry laws as they are commonly enacted.[19]

Myth: Most people think guns in the home are dangerous

Fact: 57% of Americans believe guns "protect people from becoming victims of crimes" while only 38% believe that guns "put people's safety at risk."[20]

Fact: Gallup poll concludes that 63% of Americans believe having a firearm in the home makes it safer.[21]

Fact: Sixty-eight percent of Americans would feel safer living in a neighborhood where they can own a gun rather than one where no one could have a gun for their own protection.[22]

Myth: People want local government to ban guns

Fact: Only 20% of people believe local gun control is permissible – 69% disagree.[23]

1. Bureau of Alcohol, Tobacco and Firearms, 1997
2 *Americans by Slight Margin Say Gun in the Home Makes It Safer*, Gallup Poll, October 20, 2006
3. *Public Believes Americans Have Right to Own Guns*, Gallup Poll, May 27, 2008
4. Growing Public Support for Gun Rights, Pew Research Center, December 10, 2014
5. *SAF survey of 1,015 likely voters*, Zogby, June 2002
6. ABC News, May 14, 2002
7. *Poll: More Americans oppose stricter gun control*, CNN.com, October 2015
8. *Rasmussen Reports*, February 19, 2006
9. *Less Than Half of Americans Support Stricter Gun Laws*, Gallup Poll, October 2014
10. *Rasmussen Reports*, October 05, 2009
11. *Portrait of America Survey*, August 2000
12. *Americans by Slight Margin Say Gun in the Home Makes It Safer*, Gallup Poll, October 20, 2006

13. *Americans by Slight Margin Say Gun in the Home Makes It Safer*, Gallup Poll, October 20, 2006

14. Gallup Poll Social Series: Crime, October 2013

15. *New York Times/CBS News Poll on Terrorism and the 2016 Race*, December 10, 2015

16. *Most Now Oppose an Assault Weapons Ban*, December 2015

17. New York Daily News/Rasmussen Reports national telephone survey, December 2015

18. *Majority Say More Concealed Weapons Would Make U.S. Safer*, Gallup Poll, October 2015

19. Zogby, August 4, 2009

20. Growing Public Support for Gun Rights, Pew Research Center, December 10, 2014

21. *More Than Six in 10 Americans Say Guns Make Homes Safer*, Gallop, November 2014

22. Rasmussen Reports, June 2015

23. *Rasmussen Reports*, October 05, 2009